Ufuda

one

in a million

journey to your promised land

Priscilla Shirer

LifeWay Press®. Nashville, Tennessee

Published by LifeWay Press®
© 2009 Priscilla Shirer
Reprinted July 2019

No part of this book may be reproduced or transmitted in any form or by any means, electronic
or mechanical, including photocopying and recording, or by any information storage or retrieval
system, except as my be expressly permitted in writing by the publisher. Requests for permission
should be addressed in writing to LifeWay Press ; One LifeWay Plaza; Nashville, TN 37234-0152.

ISBN: 978-1-4158-6605-4
Item 005169734

Dewey decimal classification: 248.84
Subject headings: GOD—PROMISES \ BIBLE. O.T. NUMBERS—STUDY \ CHRISTIAN LIFE

All Scripture quotations unless otherwise noted are taken from the New American Standard Bible, Copyright
© 1960, 1962, 1963, 1968, 1971, 1973, 1975, 1977, 1995 by the Lockman Foundation. Used by permission.
(www.lockman.org). Scripture quotations marked NIV are taken from the Holy Bible, New International Version,
copyright © 1973, 1978, 1984 by International Bible Society. Scripture quotations marked NLT are taken from
the Holy Bible, New Living Translation, copyright © 1996. Used by permission of Tyndale House Publishers,
Inc., Wheaton, IL 60189 USA. All rights reserved. Scripture quotations marked HCSB® are taken from the
Holman Christian Standard Bible®, © copyright 1999, 2000, 2002, 2003 by Holman Bible Publishers. Used
by permission. Scripture taken from The Message. Copyright © 1993, 1994, 1995, 1996, 2000, 2001, 2002.
Used by permission of NavPress Publishing Group. Scriptures marked ESV are from The Holy Bible, English
Standard Version (ESV) and adapted from the Revised Standard Version of the Bible, copyright Division of
Christian Education of the National Council of the Churches of Christ in the U.S.A. All rights reserved.

To order additional copies of this resource: write to LifeWay Church Resources Customer Service; One
LifeWay Plaza; Nashville, TN 37234-0113; fax 615.251.5933; phone toll free 800.458.2772; order online
at *www.lifeway.com;* email *orderentry@lifeway.com;* or visit the LifeWay Christian Store serving you.

Printed in the United States of America

Adult Ministry Publishing
LifeWay Church Resources
One LifeWay Plaza
Nashville, TN 37234-0152

CONTENTS

ABOUT THE AUTHOR

PRISCILLA SHIRER is a Bible teacher whose ministry is focused on the expository teaching of the Word of God to women. Her desire is to see women not only know the uncompromising truths of Scripture intellectually but also experience them practically by the power of the Holy Spirit. Priscilla is a graduate of Dallas Theological Seminary with a Master's degree in Biblical Studies. For over a decade she has been a conference speaker for major corporations, organizations, and Christian audiences across the United States and the world.

Priscilla is now in full-time ministry to women. She is the author of a handful of books and Bible studies including *A Jewel in His Crown* and *Discerning The Voice of God: How to Recognize When God Speaks.*

Priscilla is the daughter of pastor, speaker, and well-known author Dr. Tony Evans. She is married to her best friend Jerry and spends her days cleaning up after three fabulous boys: Jackson, Jerry Jr., and Jude. Jerry and Priscilla have founded Going Beyond Ministries, where they are committed to seeing believers receive the most out of their relationships with the Lord.

A Note From Priscilla

Welcome to *One in A Million: Journey to Your Promised Land*. I'm so thrilled that you are with me for this ride because having company makes any road trip more fun. The expedition began for me several years ago and is still in progress. God's call from mundane Christianity to a radical experience of Him has taken me down roads that, honestly, have been quite narrow.

Not many travelers have chosen to take this route. I can see why. It's easier to stay on the main road where there are more people and far less uncertainty. Besides, the travel ain't easy when you're headed in the direction of abundant living.

While I'd like to tell you that the sun has glistened on every leg of the trip and the cool winds of ease and convenience have brushed across my face without incident, I can't. On the contrary, there have been some days when I've had to take cover from the storms that life often brings. On occasion, I've had to whisper a prayer for help when loneliness knocks on my front door and comes in to stay a while. When I've met other travelers willing to brave these winding roads, our eyes have met and an instant heart connection made. Without having to say much, we've encouraged each other to continue.

I thought I knew where God was taking me when I first started out but each leg of this voyage has led into territory I've never seen before. Sometimes it's exciting and other times it's daunting. Either way, it's a ride I'd rather take with you.

I can't guarantee you much, but I can say with full confidence that you won't be bored. God's way is too unusual and mysterious for boredom to even be an option.

It's been quite a ride so far and I don't want to encounter what's next by myself.

In the next six weeks we'll traverse spiritual territory that will cover mountain peaks and deep valleys, grassy knolls and barren sand dunes, but the journey will be worth it. With the turn of each page you and I will round another corner. What we'll meet around one bend will bring a smile to the depths of our souls while others will create a sting of conviction that will send us straight to our knees. Let's be committed, OK? Buckle up and grab a venti size latte. Abundant living is at stake and I know for a fact that it's worth it!

Looking forward to taking the trip with you,

Priscilla

Session 1

Viewer Guide

Our God is a God of _____.

Yahweh was offering the children of Israel _____ in their lives.

John 10:10, "The thief comes only to steal and kill and destroy; I came that they may have life, and have it abundantly."

Of all the Jews who had the chance to experience the promised land, only _____ took God up on His offer.

Israel had been in captivity in Egypt approximately _____ _____.

There must be deliverance to even begin the journey.

Just like Israel, we need to be delivered from:

    a. A _____

    b. A _____

Israel needed deliverance from Pharaoh; we need _____ _____ _____.

In the Old Testament, the deliverer was _____. In the New Testament, the deliverer is _____ _____.

The only way to have a relationship with God is through His Son, _____ _____.

Each of us must _____ if we want to go where God is leading.

In order to get milk and honey, the Israelites had to _____ _____ from the place where Pharaoh ruled.

Galatians 5:1, "It was for freedom that Christ set us free; therefore keep standing firm and do not be subject again to a yoke of slavery."

Two questions:
1. Have you been freed from the person of the Enemy in your life?

2. Have you been freed from the places where the Enemy reigns?

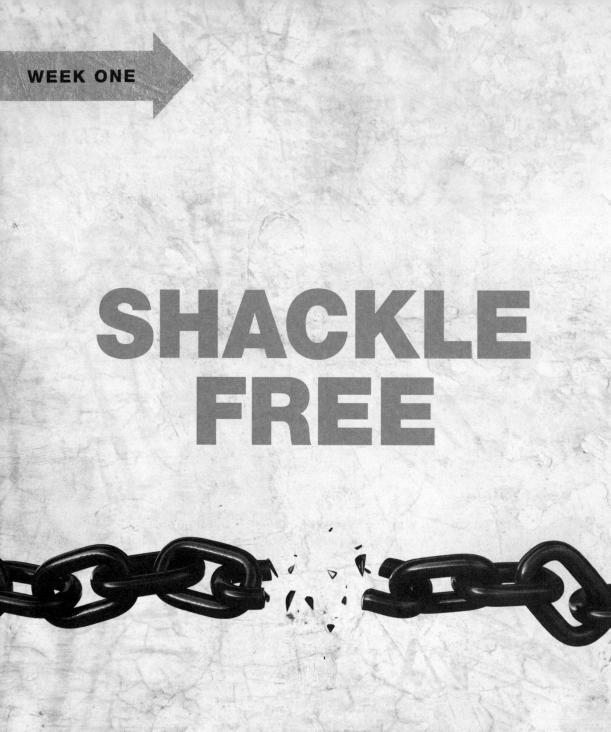

SHACKLE FREE

The show was a little long for my toddler boys. They enjoyed the circus, but as the acrobats, clowns, and other acts neared their second hour, my kids started to fidget. They'd come to see one thing: elephants.

Our family left early and piled into the car to head home. That's when we noticed an elephant eating behind a circus tent. We pulled up near the enormous beast, rolled down the windows, and gawked. This sight was just what the boys wanted!

Little was said as we watched with wide-eyed curiosity as the elephant dined. One question, however, begged to be asked. In a three-year-old's broken English my youngest voiced what we were all thinking: "How come that big ole elephant doesn't tear down this fence and escape to freedom?"

I pondered that question as I noticed the elephant glance up every now and then to peer through the fence's holes. Just beyond that wire enclosure was a whole world of activity and thrills. To me the elephant seemed to long for freedom. If only he knew that his little fence was nothing compared to his innate strength.

Day 1
Chained to a Problem

My son asked a question about the elephant that might be asked of the sheep of God's pasture (Ps. 100:3). Why don't the people of God, who can tap into so much divine power, break through the barriers that keep us from experiencing an abundant relationship with Him? Why do we hesitate to push through to freedom and abundant life?

Review the "Promised-Land Living" list on page 160. Would you say that you are currently walking in an abundant relationship to God? Why or why not?

I am not doing my part - going to church - studying Word - praying

Why do you think many believers never experience the fullness of God?

Because they put limits on god - who has none!

9

In the margin describe how the previous question applies to your experiences, past or present.

Jesus said He came to bring life in the fullest (John 10:10). Sadly, God's people often choose entrapment over the abundant life Jesus offers. Identifying what keeps us from entering into a powerful and life-altering relationship with God will help us determine how to overcome our bonds.

I pondered this question while looking at that elephant. As I watched, the animal shifted his weight and a clanking noise followed. Then I realized that hidden behind a tuft of grass, a shackle held his left ankle. I shook my head at the bolts and iron that really amounted to nothing more than an ankle bracelet on the massive beast. If only the elephant realized he could break that shackle with one powerful move and be free. To my boys, it seemed the fence kept the elephant at bay, but I knew better. That small shackle tied around his ankle was the true culprit. The elephant couldn't breach the weak fence line until he gained freedom from the chain.

Familiarize yourself with the portion of Exodus 1 in the margin. Underline the key phrases that describe the conditions the Israelites faced in bondage.

Do any areas of your life cause you to feel like the phrases you've just underlined?

GOD'S PEOPLE IN CHAINS

For about 370 years the Israelites had faced Egyptian oppression. Intimidated by their increasing numbers, Pharaoh determined to control the Hebrews by harnessing their bodies and souls. Before God's chosen people could hope to enter the land promised to them, the shackle had to break. It held them back from finding the abundance God planned for them.

Pictures in the Old Testament often foreshadow New Testament realities. Pharaoh, Egypt, Moses, and Canaan all picture realities in Christ.

Draw a line from each picture to its corresponding New Testament principle.

Pharaoh — abundant life in Christ
Egypt — life of bondage to sin
Moses — Jesus Christ
Canaan — Satan

"A new king arose over Egypt, who did not know Joseph. He said to his people, 'Behold ... the sons of Israel are more and mightier than we. Come, let us deal wisely with them, or else they will multiply and in the event of war, they will also join themselves to those who hate us, and fight against us and depart from the land.' So they appointed taskmasters over them to afflict them with hard labor. And they built for Pharaoh storage cities, Pithom and Raamses."
Exodus 1:8-11

Pharaoh's oppression of the Jews is often used to illustrate a human's oppression by Satan and bondage to sin. Satan desires to entrap each of us in a sticky web of unrepentant rebellion against God. This shackle is too tightly locked for our own fingers to pry open; only a specifically designed and uniquely appointed instrument can free us.

Before we define that instrument, let's take a closer look at the locks that fasten Satan's chains to us: The curse of sin and the lifestyle of sin. We'll explore the first today and the other tomorrow.

THE CURSE OF SIN

How does Deuteronomy 4:20 describe the conditions of Israel's bondage in Egypt? *non furnale*

What adjectives would you use to describe the life of an individual living in bondage to sin? *lonely, afraid, shackeled, separated from God — without purpose*

"The Lord has taken you and brought you out of the iron furnace, from Egypt, to be a people for His own possession, as today."
Deuteronomy 4:20

Life in slavery was brutal. In ancient times slaves generally went barefoot and their work lasted all day. In Egypt temperatures climbed to over 110 degrees. In such conditions, their kidneys suffered. Their hands were violently abused, likely torn to ribbons by the unending work. Death by dehydration, heat prostration, and heatstroke were common. To say the Israelites lived in misery is no stretch.

The harsh effects of physical slavery, however, pale in comparison to the enslaved condition of the human soul. While Israel's slavery was physical, ours originates in the depths of our hearts. Indeed, the Hebrews' hands were shredded in pain, but our souls are minced and mangled as our enemy seeks to destroy us.

The curse of sin enslaves our souls; it is a lock and chain that keeps us from finding freedom. It guarantees every human a life of separation from God.

Sin. The very word makes me cringe. Most of us prefer to use words like *indiscretion, slip,* or *mistake* to describe our souls' shortcomings. Fiery preachers of old would bellow out messages on the seriousness of sin without shame or compromise. Today the importance of calling "sin" "sin" falls to the wayside as our churches, ministries, and messages address lighter spiritual topics that draw crowds without stirring controversy. While we often skip around the very issue that most needs to be addressed, we remain shackled, peering through the fence wondering why we cannot experience true freedom. Until we deal with the shackle of sin, we cannot cross the boundaries that keep us from experiencing an abundant relationship with God.

The curse of sin began in Genesis, when Adam and Eve chose to indulge in sin in the garden of Eden. Their choice affects every human. As soon as Eve sunk her teeth into the fruit and Adam joined her rebellion, the shackle was in place and our fate was sealed. (See Gen. 3.) In an instant the curse of original sin was woven into the fabric of every life.

Adam and Eve's sin caused them to be cast from Eden, a land of endless bounty and a place where God literally walked with man in the cool of the day. Just as Adam and Eve forfeited the place of utmost fulfillment and abundance, all those who refuse to pursue freedom from the curse of sin forfeit the place of "milk and honey"—fulfillment, freedom, satisfaction, contentment, and overwhelming joy.

"Therefore, just as through one man sin entered into the world, and death through sin, and so death spread to all men, because all sinned."
Romans 5:12,
HCSB

The principle of original sin appears in Romans 5:12. Describe the curse of original sin in your own words.

one man sinned impacting the consequences on all that come behind them.

THE KEY TO FREEDOM

To obtain freedom from the shackles of Egyptian bondage, the Hebrews had to trust in God-empowered Moses as their deliverer. Moses was a uniquely appointed instrument of God, sent to deliver God's people from the rule of Pharaoh. He became a powerful symbol of God's grace. We have no record of anyone attempting to free the Israelites from Egypt until God called Moses to challenge Pharaoh.

Likewise, only One instrument can unshackle us from the curse and consequences of original sin. Just as the Israelites had to accept a fate of slavery should they choose to ignore God's plan to break their chains, we are bound to soul slavery should we ignore God's ultimate deliverer: Jesus Christ.

Read Romans 5:17-19, then complete the following.

The consequence of one transgression is *death* **(v. 17).**

The consequence of God's gift of grace through Christ is *life* **(v. 19).**

You can't afford to ignore the fact that a pit of sin separates you from the Father. Your journey toward abundance and fullness must start at the foot of the cross.

If, like me, you are ready to experience God, not just know about Him, make certain that you are no longer under the curse of original sin.

If you have accepted reconciliation with God through the death and resurrection of Christ, write the time and circumstances surrounding your commitment. Solidify that decision through prayer.

high school at campus crusade for Christ

If you aren't sure that you've ever taken this step, then why stay shackled for another day? Abundance and fullness of life are just beyond the bend! Take time to accept God's gift of Jesus Christ! It's simple. See Romans 10:9. Then consider writing the following prayer in your own words as you give your life to Christ. (Don't forget to share your decision with your group leader or another friend in your study. She'll be thrilled!)

Lord Jesus, I am a sinner in need of a Savior. I no longer want to be bound by the curse of sin. I want to be free. I believe You are the only One who can accomplish this in my life. I accept Your death on Calvary as payment for my sins. Today I place faith in You as the only way, the only truth, and the only life (John 14:6). Please, Jesus, take up residence in me through the Person of the Holy Spirit to empower me to walk fully in the abundance that You desire. In Jesus' name, amen.

"If you confess with your mouth, 'Jesus is Lord,' and believe in your heart that God raised Him from the dead, you will be saved."
Romans 10:9

Day 2
Chained By Choice

The image of the chained elephant haunted me long after we left the circus. A Google™ search helped answer some of my questions. I discovered they train elephants by chaining them in infancy. Since the babies are not strong enough to pull free, they grow tired of trying and resign themselves to a life of limitations. They adapt to living in boundaries of the chain. Soon even a small rope is sufficient to restrain an enormous elephant. The animal considers freedom a hopeless notion and therefore stops trying to experience it.

Yesterday we discovered that by God's grace through Jesus we can be free from the curse of original sin. Once a relationship with God has been established through Christ, the journey to freedom begins. Before we can travel to our personal Canaan with any effectiveness, however, we must also overcome a second lock that fastens the Enemy's chain to us: the sinful lifestyle.

In what ways do you think lifestyle sin differs from original sin? *we are all born with original sin lifestyle sin is a choice*

Overcoming original sin requires that we accept God's gracious gift of His Son, who overcame sin's powerful hold over people. Overcoming a sinful lifestyle, on the other hand, requires daily relying on the Holy Spirit's power. It means that we must continually turn our backs on the temptation to rebel against God.

"It was for freedom that Christ set us free; therefore keep standing firm and do not be subject again to a yoke of slavery."
Galatians 5:1

Underline the section of Galatians 5:1 that reveals Christ's work for us. Circle our responsibility.

A difference exists between being free in Christ and living free in Him. After Pharaoh agreed to free the slaves, the children of Israel had to make a choice to pack their bags, physically leave, and follow Moses to Canaan. I remember times when I complained that my Christian life didn't seem to have any of the "milk and honey" that the Lord offered in Scripture. Thinking back, those times have corresponded to seasons when my lifestyle was not matching up with my God-given position.

What a tragedy it would be for us to be given freedom but not walk in it! For believers, the ability to walk in freedom becomes dependent on an individual's daily decision to walk in the power received at salvation.

> **Describe a time when you lived as a slave to sin even though you were a free believer. How did you feel?**

overeating, buying gossip. Knew God was disappointed in me

We must change the sinful ways we've been trained to live and by the Holy Spirit's power within us, we can. The only way to deprogram an elephant so that he no longer enjoys captivity but experiences and enjoys freedom is to unfetter him and gently guide him into the wild. Since our tendency as humans is to err in a direction away from God, we must retrain ourselves to walk in the ways of freedom.

> **Prepare to brainstorm in your group practical ways we can reprogram our thinking to fully enjoy God's freedom.**

surround yourself with Christian friends. pray constantly study His word. Praise accountability partner

LIVING FREE

The Enemy wants to keep us from living free. God gives believers in Christ positional sanctification. That means we have a position of "set-apartness," holiness and righteousness that cannot be altered or manipulated. Nothing can be done to remove a true believer from her positional standing of righteousness before the Father. Being positionally sanctified, however, cannot be the end goal of a believer determined to live in Christ's freedom.

After our standing before the Father is secured, we must turn our attention to the business of lifestyle sanctification, leaving Egypt behind us. Since we still live in the flesh, which has sinful tendencies, and since we have an enemy who is working against us, we must work through a process that requires obedience and yieldedness to God. Being declared free gives us eternal freedom but walking in it gives us daily freedom. Although salvation is definitely by faith and not works, daily living in that freedom takes work as we cooperate with God's Spirit.

It's important to note that Pharaoh had difficulty managing the abundant number of Israelites. He acknowledged this by appointing taskmasters over them. These taskmasters served a sinister purpose.

Look carefully at Exodus 1:11-14, and in the margin list words or phrases that reveal the taskmasters' role.

Verse 12 uses the word afflict. The Hebrew word used here is *anah*, the same word used in Genesis 15:13 to describe the oppression God's people would face.[1] This word means "to thwart, to frustrate, to be made low, to be bowed down and made submissive."[2] In other words, the goal of Egyptian slavery was not merely physical. Egyptian rulers intended to demolish the spirit of the Hebrew people, thereby lessening any threat of rebellion or escape. This kind of abuse undoubtedly helped to dissuade the children of God from desiring to live like the people of God.

We must recognize that the Devil has assigned taskmasters to us too. The Enemy of our souls knows our strengths and weaknesses, and he has the goal of contriving ways to keep us under his thumb. He wants to burden each of us to the point that we no longer feel passionate about being people of God. He does it by convincing us that freedom in Christ is a dream. He encourages us to keep returning to the very sins from which Christ freed us. The writer of Hebrews warns of this: "Let us also lay aside every encumbrance and the sin which so easily entangles us" (12:1). Notice the passage says "the" sin—it's a specific and personal affliction that is unique to you.

With what specific "affliction" is the Devil plaguing you right now?

THE MIND GAME

In part living in freedom depends on our response to the Devil's mind games. A mind game of sorts holds the elephant at the circus captive: Feel the chain around your leg? No freedom for you! The Enemy plays a similar trick on us. He causes us to think that freedom is impossible. By getting us mired in a lifestyle of sin, he makes us feel hopeless. It's not long before we give up on the idea of really experiencing God in our lives. We begin to think that liberty from life's messes is more fiction than fact.

One key method Satan uses to keep us captive is by causing us to gradually step further and further into our rebellion. Eventually we are deeper than we ever thought we'd be.

Sin is progressive. What once satisfied us loses its power. Before we know it we are more and more entangled in a web that is slowly taking the life out of us. The situation the Hebrews faced illustrates the progression. The moment Moses breathed the freedom concept over their lives, Pharaoh upped the ante. (See Ex. 5:7-11.)

What is it like to have your sin snowball out of control?

Are you caught in a lifestyle of sin you just can't seem to shake? The Enemy's goal is to keep you in his web so you can never journey toward the soul-cleansing freedom the Lord has for you. End today's lesson by offering yourself to the Lord and honestly exposing your rebellion, discouragement, and fatigue to Him. Ask the Lord to help you share your struggle with another believer who can keep you accountable on the journey to living free.

Day 3
Bound to a Memory

In 1863 President Lincoln issued the Emancipation Proclamation. The document consisted of two executive orders leading to freedom for four million slaves who lived on American soil. The news of legal freedom was met with unbridled joy by those inflicted by inhumane treatment under slavery. Not all slaves, though, rejoiced at the announcement.

The problem was that many slaves had come to enjoy their lifestyles compared to the ominous alternatives. "House slaves," for example, worked directly with their master's families. They were often granted far superior treatment to that experienced by field slaves. Relatively speaking, a house slave's life was simple and fairly convenient. It came with certain perks that some weren't certain they wanted to leave behind. To some, experiencing freedom would mean losing a life far from ideal but at least less risky than the unknown. Many house slaves willingly chose slavery over freedom to avoid the risks that freedom entailed. This begs the question: Were they really free?

Far too often the decision made by some post-war slaves reflects the choices of modern Christians. For the remainder of this week, let's turn our consideration to another potential barrier to experiencing promised-land living in Christ: an addiction to the "perks" of sin.

What are some of the perks you've seen the Enemy attach to sin to make it more appealing?

17

one

> "The rabble who were among them had greedy desires; and also the sons of Israel wept again and said, 'Who will give us meat to eat? We remember the fish which we used to eat free in Egypt, the cucumbers and the melons and the leeks and the onions and the garlic, but now our appetite is gone. There is nothing at all to look at except this manna.' Now the manna was like coriander seed, and its appearance like that of bdellium."
>
> Numbers 11:4-7

CLINGING TO THE CHAINS

Much like the 1800s slaves who balked at leaving behind relative comforts, the Israelites grumbled at their loss of perceived "privileges." After they were freed and followed Moses into the wilderness toward the promised land, they began longing for some of the comforts of Egypt.

Read Numbers 11:4-7. What did the Israelites leave behind and what had God given them instead?

food they knew   *manna that they didn't know*

The Israelites had to leave behind a few slavery "perks"—not the least of which was the assurance of nourishment. Freedom was risky. It meant daily trusting in God to provide what they needed. In Egypt they knew where their bread and butter … ummm … fish and garlic were coming from; even better, they knew they were indeed coming. As the Hebrews followed Moses through the desert they had no such assurance.

For the Hebrews, security and comfort came from knowing how their next meal was going to be provided and that it was going to consist of familiar flavors. As they longed for that security and wanted to return to the very place from where they'd just been freed, Pharaoh ceased to be their worst enemy. They became their own!

Recall a time when you became your own worst enemy. What did you say or think that impeded your spiritual progress?

Sometimes the adversary is no longer our worst enemy. Neither the curse nor the lifestyle of sin holds us back. Instead, our own fear of walking in freedom begins to cripple us. In a sense, we start to partner with our captor in his attempt to keep us enslaved and away from abundance and fullness in God.

Describe in the margin how the strong flavors and smells of Egypt's food contributed to Israel's bondage and how this tendency might apply to you.

College was not a good time in my spiritual life. Although the Lord has graciously used much of my rebellion to teach me valuable lessons, I admit those days were filled with staunch stubbornness against Him. Some of the activities I participated in and relationships I indulged in repulse me now. Yet frequently the Enemy attempts to remind me of the "perks" of my Egypt. The bold flavor of freedom and strong spice of a lack of responsibility associated with college days often lurk in my mind. If I'm not careful I can easily wallow in a longing for the "fish and garlic" of my Egypt, neglecting the current nourishment God provides.

EATING AT THE ENEMY'S TABLE

Let's be honest: Life estranged from God has fleshly perks. The Enemy of our soul always ensures that we enjoy at least a portion of our sin. He makes certain the enjoyment is addictive. The onions, leeks, garlic, fish, and melon that satisfied and gratified our flesh for so long were nice at the time. We enjoyed them; in fact, they helped content us with slavery. But to accept God's call to journey onward means some things must also be left behind, even the things that tempt us to return to the old ways.

Interesting how just a few perks could make an entire group of people forget the hardships of slavery. Our Enemy is crafty. He allows us just enough nourishment to blind us to the brutality of spiritual slavery. The Egyptians fed the Hebrews to give them strength to build for Pharaoh (Ex. 1:11). We can be sure that any good things the Enemy gives us are only intended to keep us nourished enough to continue under the yoke of his bondage.

One thing worse than slavery is slavery with addictive perks.

Why do you think we get so attached to the perks the Enemy gives while developing spiritual amnesia about the hardship involved? *unknown is scary, instant gratification*

Think of an "Egypt" time when you were living in rebellion against God. On the left side of the chart write one of those circumstances. On the right, write the corresponding "perk" the Enemy gave you. I've given you an example.

Egypt's hardships	Egyptian perk
fear of being caught in an affair	spontaneity, fun, little responsibility
gossip	

Do you think more of the hardship or the perk when you consider your time there? Why?

The lure of eating at Pharaoh's table often stands in the way of a believer fully engaging in a journey to live abundantly in Christ. Our Enemy aspires to keep our minds on Egypt instead of the destination God has for us—the land flowing with milk and honey.

"We remember the fish which we used to eat free in Egypt, the cucumbers and the melons and the leeks and the onions and the garlic."
Numbers 11:5

Look carefully at Numbers 11:5 As the children of Israel complained they mentioned the fish. Though this fish might not have cost them earned wages, why was it certainly not free?

"Perks" are not necessarily ungodly things. They can be, but nothing is inherently wrong with the desire to taste the foods that tickled their memories. The problem was they wanted those things more than they wanted the new thing God was providing for them. This tendency revealed their continued attachment to the very things from which Yahweh had freed them.

My Sister, if you want to experience the fullness of all that God has to offer you, you must make a tough decision. Will you let go of sin's perks in order to follow the Holy Spirit to spiritual abundance? The initial separation might be difficult, but not making the choice will ensure that you never live in true freedom and experience abundant life.

What specific things is God asking you to leave behind so you can more closely follow Him?

Take time to honestly admit your heart's longing for anything the Enemy uses to keep you chained to sin. Offer those things to the Lord. Ask God to give you holy boldness and courage by His Spirit to break the hold those "perks" have on you. Commit to God's new menu for you.

Rest assured, God's meal will be better suited to your palate than anything your time in Egypt could provide.

Day 4

A Little of This; A Little of That

My heart has a soft spot for the food my South American mother prepares. Growing up, I had an aversion to it. It was spicy and soupy. Everything was made in gravy filled with a variety of Caribbean flavors. My young taste buds couldn't handle it. Now things are different. After years of feasting on the treats of my mother's home, I'm not only used to them but long for them. When the holidays roll around, I sit on the edge of my seat waiting for the delectable curried meats, spicy vegetables, and steamy peas and rice. I even spoon on hot sauce for more pepper action! Anything less than these intense flavors piled together now falls short of my idea of holiday eating.

The Hebrews longed for the tastes of Egypt. What about those foods seemed so appealing? We can't answer that question without first acknowledging the dramatic diet change that followed the exodus. The days of plentiful and varied diets of international fare were gone. God whittled the menu down to one dish.

How would you feel if your diet were suddenly limited to one unfamiliar dish?

Using Numbers 11:6, summarize the Israelites' feelings about their new menu.

not hungry enough to eat if

"Now our appetite is gone. There is nothing at all to look at except this manna."
Numbers 11:6

Manna, apparently a bread-like substance, was the foundation of the Israelites' menu for 40 years! Numbers 11:8-9 explains that when the dew fell on the camp at night, the manna fell with it. Daily the people would pick it up and prepare it. Baked manna. Fried manna. Sautéed manna. Manna soufflé, manna casserole. Manna in the morning. Manna in the evening. The sameness of the situation is most assuredly what led the children of Israel, long fed on pagan bounty, to turn up their noses at this seemingly dull display of heavenly provision.

I want to give the children of Israel the benefit of the doubt. I can understand how it may have been difficult for Hebrew taste buds not to long for the varying foods to which they had become accustomed. I'm a woman who appreciates variety in my diet. For goodness sake, eating is my favorite hobby! But we must understand that their desire for Egyptian variety is symbolic of our longing for the variety of foreign behaviors to which we have become accustomed. Far too many Christians turn away from the narrow road of abundant living to temporarily enjoy the Enemy's worldly variety.

Yesterday, I turned on a top-rated show to find the day's discussion being led by a self-proclaimed spiritual guru. He offered the captive studio audience a variety of options they could use to tap into "God." "Come to God any way you want and through any means" was his bold declaration. "Jesus Christ is only a way to connect to God, certainly not the way." The crowd nodded, smiled, applauded, and received the "food" of Egypt on a silver platter. Christianity's foundational principle that only our Savior, Jesus Christ, connects us with God seems a bit limited in a world flooded with colorful, aromatic options like "you can be your own God" and "God is a relative concept."

List ways the Enemy's offer of variety works against God's simple gift of Christ in our culture. Which most affects you? your family? your church?

Brainstorm ways to guard yourself and your family from these trends. Plan to discuss them with your group.

Like the Egyptians, we fall prey to the idea that Egypt's table overflows with delectable treats. The truth, however, is that we can enjoy true spiritual freedom only when we commit to accepting the pure, daily bread God provides.

The simplicity and singleness of the manna in the wilderness symbolized the Christ who was to come. When presenting Himself as the true Messiah to the Jews Jesus clearly said, "I am the bread of life" (John 6:35). While the manna of the wilderness could not provide eternal life, Christ did and will to anyone who will receive it.

Heaven's manna was God's miraculous portion given to the children of Israel, not to bore them but to show them a new dimension of Him. This portion is given to us just as freely as He gave it the Israelites.

CLEANSING OUR PALATES

Egypt's variety wasn't Israel's only problem. They had trouble adapting to manna's simplicity as well. To the Hebrew children Egypt's food seemed far more exciting than God's, and this distortion of God's goodness always results in grumbling and complaining. It emphasizes the meager benefits of Egypt over the grand and thrilling blessings of God. Consider the intense flavors of the six food options they mentioned in Numbers 11:5. Most of them have flavors so pungent that their odor lingers for hours! A mixture of different Egyptian spices, flavors, and meal choices no doubt altered the Hebrews' taste buds.

> **Read Exodus 16:31 and Numbers 11:8. How do these passages describe manna?**

heavenly, honey, cakes baked w/ oil

Manna was really anything but boring. "It looked like bdellium (v. 7), a prized substance that was one of the products of the area immediately surrounding the Garden of Eden (Genesis 2:12)."[3] The Holman Christian Standard Bible gives a more realistic description of manna: "It tasted like a pastry cooked with the finest oil" (Num. 11:8). It may have looked somewhat like porridge, but it actually tasted more like Krispy Kreme® donuts.

Manna was "the bread of heaven" (Ps. 78:24, NKJV), the original angelfood cake! Their grumbling caused them to overlook the tasty treasure they'd been given.

> **What do you complain about most in the journey God has you on? List five good things about your journey that complaining has caused you to overlook.**
> 1.
> 2.
> 3.
> 4.
> 5.

The contrast between Egypt's food and God's gift of manna is stark, isn't it? The purity of the manna stands out against Egypt's menu. God gave this meal as a gift to His people, not only to sustain them in their journey but also to wean the Hebrews off their accustomed tastes. God seemed eager, didn't He, to begin the process of taking the desire for Egypt out of the mouths of the ones He loves? To start living like free men and women, His people have to start eating like them.

"The house of Israel named it manna, and it was like coriander seed, white, and its taste was like wafers with honey."
Exodus 16:31

"The people would go about and gather it and grind it between two millstones or beat it in the mortar, and boil it in the pot and make cakes with it; and its taste was as the taste of cakes baked with oil."
Numbers 11:8

one

in a million

Consider the last sentence in the preceding paragraph. How might John 6:35 impact how we see the manna?

FOREIGN FOODS

The Enemy wants us to feed on things that will cause our stomachs to turn at the thought of pure devotion to Christ. He wants us to miss the variety and spice that a life bound in sin offers. He wants us to long for it even after we've made a decision to journey with God. As long as we keep complaining about what we have now and longing for what the Devil once "gave" us, our journey with the Lord will be stop-and-go at best.

I believe this principle was foremost in Daniel's mind when he refused the rich food of Babylon. King Nebuchadnezzar brought in the finest of Israel's youth, Daniel among them, so he could indoctrinate them in the pagan ways of Babylon. The king did everything to get Israel and Israel's God off the minds of these young men. To reprogram them, Nebuchadnezzar had his servants teach the literature and languages of the Chaldeans. He made them drink wines and eat foods prepared with signature Babylonian spices. He even had their names changed so they would be continually reminded of their new connection with Babylon and of the expected change in their devotion to Yahweh. Daniel 1:8 records his response to the king's order that he eat the rich food of Babylon.

Why do you think Daniel chose to rebel on what surely seemed to some a minor issue given his circumstances?

Nebuchadnezzar's advisors feared Daniel's refusal would be easily evidenced in his lack of strength and physical prowess, but Daniel challenged them. He requested simple meals of vegetables and water while other men continued to feast on the flavorful meals of the culture. God honored Daniel and his friends' integrity not only physically but mentally and spiritually. He "gave them knowledge and intelligence in every branch of literature and wisdom; Daniel even understood all kinds of visions and dreams" (Dan. 1:17).

When we accept Christ and lean on Him to help us move past the lifestyle sins that entrap us, you and I are free of Egypt. We must, however, be on the alert for the Enemy's continual attempts to rename us, to retrain us, and to readapt us to his way of thinking, speaking, acting, and living. Like Daniel, we must adapt a strong resolve and a firm stand against Satan's attempts to serve us food from his table.

Consider in which of your activities you can see the Enemy's attempt to fill you with his ideas, philosophies, and ideologies. In the margin note specific things you can do to thwart his efforts.

May we desire God's ways above all else. May our hearts ring with the song of David in Psalm 84:1-2: "How lovely are Your dwelling places, O LORD of hosts! My soul longed and even yearned for the courts of the LORD; My heart and my flesh sing for joy to the living God."

Day 5
God In a Box

I sat across from a woman I'd only just met and almost instantly the Spirit drew us together. Our conversation turned to deep spiritual matters only moments after our first "hello." We had the same sound background of theological training and had both learned from Bible teachers who taught with clarity the principles of Scripture that were now well ingrained into our personal lives and ministries. Yet we were both parched—thirsty for more and it was this thirst that brought us to our knees in a hotel room. With deeply moving worship music playing in the background, she began to share the gripping story of how God had placed in her a holy hunger for more than just a simple knowledge of Him but an experience with Him through the Spirit of God. She told me that this hunger had gotten her into trouble as she began to experience things that were outside of the box.

I could relate. I've attended a Bible-based church my entire life. The teaching I receive is unbelievably edifying, and I credit it with any foundational knowledge I have about the Scriptures. Yet just like my new friend, the Lord had whetted my spiritual appetite for a more personal relationship with Him.

Through a series of events, God has invited me to expect and anticipate more out of my walk with Him. My journey to promised land living began because He placed a gnawing hunger in my heart to encounter the God I knew so much about. With each divine interruption in my life and in my theology, I received a golden sealed invitation to see God outside of the box. He wants me to expect to see His power in supernatural ways, anticipate miracles in my everyday existence and hear His voice with startling clarity.

As I consider what we've studied this week, it occurs to me that one more thing keeps us from journeying with God into a life that flows with the Holy Spirit's power—a narrow view of God creates a boundary that limits our experience of Him. For me, the comforts of my upbringing, church, and scholastic training began to create a wall between me and abundant living.

> God's work in us thus far isn't a box into which He will fit, but a slab upon which He will build.

The teaching I received was not biblically incorrect; on the contrary, it was solid and effective. But what I was given in knowledge, God wanted to expand through experience. He wanted the Word to become "spirit and life" to me (John 6:63). I asked God for an open heart and courage to receive whatever He had for me. He graciously responded by supplementing my membership at my home church with a Bible study group filled with people from completely different backgrounds. This group hungered to experience the truths of Scripture. They expected God's supernatural activity and seeing it was a normal part of their fellowship and personal lives.

I believe the failure to be open to a larger view of God often hinders church-going, Bible-study-doing women like you and me. We must be willing to move out of our comfort zones and church routines if we are to break through to the abundant life Christ offers. By no means am I suggesting that you discontinue fellowship with the church God has you in now. I merely want you to consider that there may be others the Lord might want to use to assist you on your journey. The following three case studies consider God-fearing women at a crossroads of faith. To move past stalemates in their relationships with the Lord, each of the ladies needs to make some changes.

Read each scenario, and then in the margin write what you think each woman should do to move ahead in her relationship with God.

Case 1: Leslie is a young businesswoman. As she has matured spiritually, she has realized that many of the traditions taught by her strict, legalistic denomination and well-meaning parents don't coincide with the truth of Scripture. What should Leslie do to make sure she keeps moving ahead in her relationship with the Lord?

Case 2: Mrs. Gonzales is a stay-at-home grandma. In the past three years God has shown her some miraculous evidence of His activity in her life. Her home church condemns supernatural activity as unconventional or even fanatical. She senses that the teaching of her church is generally theologically sound but narrow. She cannot deny what God is doing in her life. How can Michelle continue to advance in her walk with God?

Case 3: Kylie is an aspiring model. She was raised to embrace the supernatural and to believe that prosperity belongs to every believer. Her walk with God allows her to see that the teaching she receives sometimes emphasizes experience and emotion over truth. What steps can Kylie take to make sure her relationship with the Lord is on the right track?

remember truth to priority

With which woman's story do you most relate? Why?

Kylie

"Don't let church obscure your view of God." Tommy Tenny, *The God Catchers Workbook*

Leslie, Michelle, and Kylie recognize that God offers them something different in their relationship with Him than what they've previously known. If your advice to the ladies revolved around digging in the Word, developing a deeper prayer life, or even searching for a supplemental body of believers with which to grow, you are on the right track. In all cases, the women must step out of the cozy comfort zones of their pasts to accept God's invitation to journey onward. When we sense the unmistakable stirring of the Holy Spirit beckoning us to a deeper walk, we have to make decisions that stretch us.

Has church/ministry ever obscured your view of God? If so, explain.

Where do you sense God leading you that is different from where you have been up until this point?

Fear of change and the desire to avoid challenge often stand in the way of a believer's growing into an experiential relationship with God. This, in fact, is what caused the vast majority of those led out of Egypt to die in the desert instead of the promised land. Out of the original multitude who fled Pharaoh, only two remained faithful to obeying God, willingly accepting what God laid before them. Joshua and Caleb were willing to leave the comfortable majority for a chance to draw closer to God.

Fear of change and the desire to avoid challenge often stand in the way of a believer's growth.

RABBLE ROUSING

I believe one key to moving forward efficiently in our journey with God rests in the company we keep (and yes, that includes "church company"). Those who want to grow with God need to deeply search the Word and have an openness to experience Him in new ways, but Numbers 11 suggests that those with whom we share fellowship can easily become a stumbling block to us in our desire to walk with the Lord.

Read Numbers 11:1-4 and answer the following questions.

What group of people seemed to stir dissension in the Israelite camp?

What caused them to complain?

How did their actions affect the Jews?

Israel's frustration with desert life was inflamed by their affiliation with a group of people the Scriptures call "the rabble." These were the "riff-raff" who lived on the outskirts of the camp. They were a "mixed multitude of all nationalities who came out of Egypt with God's people but had never fully assimilated and taken on Israel's values and standards."[5] These people were free from all of the bondage of Egypt but were not fully engaged in God's calling on His people to follow after Him. Their halfheartedness swept like a forest fire through the camp, infecting God's people with indifference toward God. The grumbling was contagious.

According to Numbers 11:10, the complaints had a ripple effect. Check all that apply.
- [ ] **God's anger was roused.**
- [ ] **Scorpions and vipers attacked the camp.**
- [ ] **Moses' displeasure grew.**
- [ ] **Return to Egypt became inevitable.**
- [ ] **General contentment reigned throughout the camp.**

What type of company do you keep? Do your closest relationships consist of "the rabble," those who are saved and freed from the Enemy's hold but who only halfheartedly pursue God's fullness? Or are they men and women who passionately pursue God's heart, even at the expense of encountering unmapped territory? Do your friends' presence arouse in you a pursuit for more of God? Do their experiences with God excite your passion to have encounters of your own?

On the left side of the chart list the names of the five people (other than your spouse and children) with whom you spend the most time. On the right side describe the effect each person's spiritual life has on yours.

#	Name	Effect
1	Stacy	strong believer - example serious
2	Joanna	non-believer
3	Judy	strong believer example - serious
4	Dianne	Catholic - staunch
5	Beth	believer - not strong

One of the most gracious things the Lord has done for me Is to strategically place individuals in my life who help me on my journey into Canaan. My connection with associates who aren't serious about experiencing God have waned, and I am carefully holding fast to those whose pursuit of God encourages my own. I call them my "wild women." These are ladies who pray and then believe. They ask and then expect. When my questions need answers, these women provide a safe place where I will not be judged as I explore the depths of God and His work in me. Using the truth of God's Word and the maturity gained in their own experiences, they guide me.

Maybe in your Bible study group there are women whose hearts are burning just like yours is. Together you can encourage each other to fully pursue God's work.

Write a prayer asking the Lord to help you make wise decisions regarding your relationships. Ask Him to bring people into your life who will encourage you and foster your pursuit of God as you press onward to abundant life.

1. John F. Walvoord and Roy B. Zuck. *The Bible Knowledge Commentary,* (Wheaton, IL: Victor Books, 1985), 1:55.
2. Francis Brown et. al. *Enhanced Brown-Driver-Briggs Hebrew and English Lexicon* (electronic ed.) (Oak Harbor, WA: Logos Research Systems, 2000), xiii.
3. Iain M. Duguid. *Numbers: God's Presence in the Wilderness* (Wheaton, IL: Crossway Books, 2006), 150.
4. Tommy Tenney. *The God Catchers Workbook: Experiencing the Manifest Presence of God* (Nashville: Thomas Nelson, 2001), 56.
5. Duguid, 148.

Session 2
Viewer Guide

Exodus 13:17
"Now when Pharaoh had let the people go, God did not lead them by the way of the land of the Philistines, even though it was near; for God said, 'The people might change their minds when they see war, and return to Egypt.'"

God _chose_ the wilderness for the people of Israel.

challenge was not a mistake ~ he chose the wilderness for those he loved the most

There are some things we don't know about ourselves until we are put in a position where we have to see God's power _working_ _through us_.

God will _comfort_ us by His Holy Spirit. _Trust_ Him with the wilderness.

God wants to develop us, and He uses the wilderness to do it.

When we get eye to eye w/challenge we gets to see the supernatural of god we wouldn't otherwise "wilderness" is your life when you've been de railed

The wilderness is god's choice for our life. Its a time we need to trust Him that He wants us to see something about ourselves and His intimacy

Job 42:5
**"I have heard of You by the hearing of the ear;
But now my eye sees You."** *This is what wilderness is all about*

You can't see miracles unless there is an ___*impossible*___
___*situation*___ you can't figure out for yourself.

*wilderness -
to see Him more intimately*

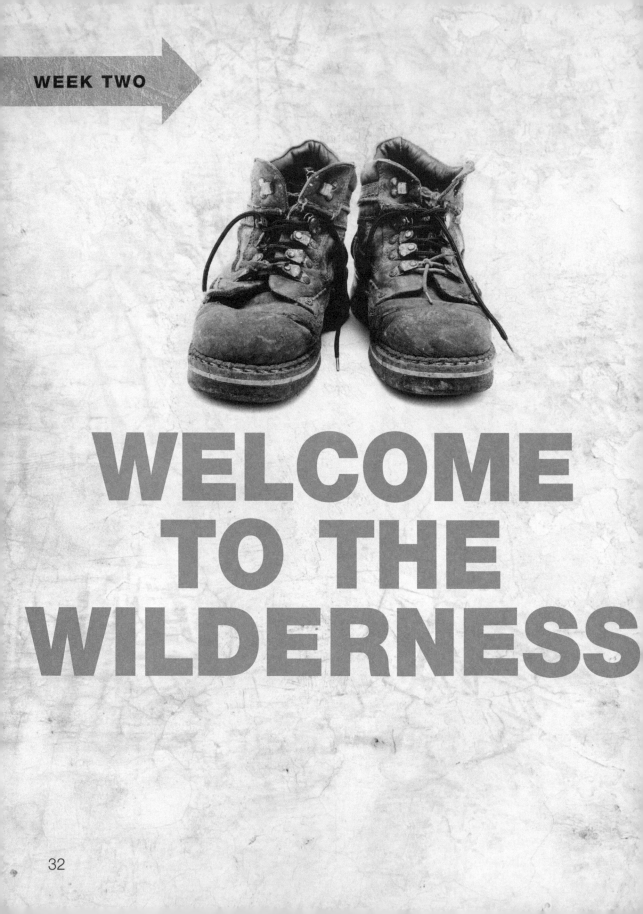

Day 1
The Dry and Dusty Wilderness

If you've made a decision with me to leave Egypt and fully embrace the journey with God, I have a warning: This journey will not be easy. It will test your faith, stretch your belief system, and challenge your level of commitment—but onward we must go. We know that God's destination will be filled with everything we need and so much of what we want. Is it worth this difficult journey? Absolutely!

List some difficulties you are facing in your life as you journey with God right now.

Examine the map (back of the book). Familiarize yourself with the major stops on Israel's journey.

Draw a line on the map to show the most direct route between Egypt and Canaan.

The Israelites probably left Egypt in anticipation of a fairly short journey. The highway along the coast of the Mediterranean Sea would appear their obvious and most efficient escape route. "From Israel's present location on the east side of the [Red Sea] to southern Canaan was approximately 150 miles, which, had the people gone directly, would have taken less than a month to traverse."[1] Knowing this, the people surely prepared mentally and physically for a camping and hiking adventure lasting 30 days or less.

Exodus 13:17-18 explains that what seemed the best freedom path to the Hebrews would have caused trials that they were not ready to face.

Read these verses in the margin. Who led the Hebrews? *God*

Where did He lead them? *The wilderness*

Why?

> *"Now when Pharaoh had let the people go, God did not lead them by the way of the land of the Philistines, even though it was near; for God said, 'The people might change their minds when they see war, and return to Egypt.' Hence God led the people around by the way of the wilderness to the Red Sea; and the sons of Israel went up in martial array from the land of Egypt."*
> **Exodus 13:17-18**

The Lord often chooses a wilderness experience for us because His goal is to make us more dependent on Him.

Note that the Hebrews didn't just happen upon the wilderness. Their GPS didn't malfunction. God led them there, directing their steps according to His divine plan (see Ex. 14:1-4). When lifted against the backdrop of our own standards, thoughts, and expectations, the road God chooses for us is often not the road we might expect. He often chooses a wilderness journey for us to give us an opportunity to experience Him in a way we might miss in a place of ease and convenience.

> **When wilderness seasons come in your life or a friend's life, what or who do you assume to be the source?**
> ▢ sin   ▢ the Enemy
> ▢ God   ▢ coincidence
> ▢ other: _____

THE WILDERNESS OF PURPOSE

"Then they set out from Succoth and camped in Etham on the edge of the wilderness."
Exodus 13:20

On the map draw a circle around Etham.

God led the people to camp in Etham to prepare for their wilderness trek. According to Exodus 13:20, Etham was at the edge of the wilderness, in the opposite direction of the northern route they thought they would take. Imagine the Israelites' thoughts as they pondered the vast wasteland before them.

> **Put yourself in the Hebrews' sandals. How would you feel if facing the desert on foot when a more convenient route obviously existed?**

From Etham Israel had a clear view of the vast and dry wilderness stretching before them. They could see the difficulty they'd face if God continued to move them in that direction. Their hearts probably palpitated with anxiety as they considered their future. With Egypt behind them and a wilderness before them, they had to do a heart check. Would they follow God even if the way was difficult? Only wholehearted devotion would ensure their entry into the promised land.

I believe Etham describes the place where God gives a vision of what's coming. It's the place of final decision where He lets us camp out to consider the challenge ahead. Whether He's asking us to stay in a rough marriage, to mother difficult children, to accept singleness, to choose full-time ministry, to let go of friendships, to suffer illness, or to navigate a situation we feel we can't survive, we have to decide if we will follow where He is leading and trust that He knows what He is doing. Etham is the place where you don't know all of the details of the life God is choosing, but a quick look at the tumbleweed blowing across the landscape lets you know it will be dry.

Does God have you camped at an "Etham" right now?
☐ yes   ☐ no   ☐ not sure

In the margin describe a personal "Etham" where you found yourself questioning God's direction in your life. How might Isaiah 55:8 encourage you the next time you find yourself camped in Etham?

"For My thoughts are not your thoughts, Nor are your ways My ways," declares the LORD.
Isaiah 55:8

God is mysterious and His ways unusual. When seen against the backdrop of our own standards, thoughts, and expectations, the road God chooses to lead us as we travel into a life of abundance with Him is most assuredly not the road we would have chosen for ourselves. Sometimes His way is:

| more challenging | more tedious | more indirect |
| more lonely | more costly | |

In the margin list what you would add to this list.

Travel through the wilderness protected the Israelites from military encounters that would've sent them running back to Egypt. It positioned them to see an incredible miracle. You can be certain that God is looking out for your greater good, too. First Peter 1:6-7 elaborates: "You may have had to suffer grief in all kinds of trials. These have come so that your faith—of greater worth than gold, which perishes even though refined by fire—may be proven genuine and may result in praise, glory and honor" (NIV).

How does the fact that our trials have purpose alter your view of God's care? Check one.
☐ It doesn't; I've always believed God is in control of all.
☐ It amazes me that God can bring good out of difficulty.
☐ I wonder why I'm so determined to give my kids the best of everything when God sometimes chooses difficulties as the best teaching tools for me, His child.
☐ I think it's great, but I'd still rather go through life without tough times.
☐ other: _____

"I know, O LORD, that a man's way is not in himself, Nor is it in a man who walks to direct his steps."
Jeremiah 10:23

A VISION OF GOD IN THE DRY AND DUSTY

The dry and dusty wilderness Israel faced undoubtedly made for an uncomfortable journey, but the Lord assigned it because He saw the end result.

The idea of wilderness living best illustrates how God allows and uses difficulty to His children's greater good. Job's story elaborates on this principle. Job was a "blameless, upright [man], fearing God and turning away from evil" (Job 1:1). He relished a life complete with a caring family and more money than he could spend. Job sat comfortably within the "hedge" God provided around all he owned (1:10). Yet the Lord allowed Satan to attack Job's comfortable existence, and the Devil went at him full force.

One day invaders attacked Job's fields, took his oxen, and killed his servants. In the same breath a fire burned up his sheep and killed even more of his servants. Scripture also reports that Job's camels were raided, a move likely wiping out what had once been an impressive number of livestock. But the news only grew worse: A tornado struck the house in which his children dined. All were lost. Soon Job's health was so bad that even his friends couldn't recognize him (2:12). Boils covered his skin, and he sat in an ash heap.

Job's story is a clear account of a man who loved God and was loved by God, yet his life became a wilderness of frustration and loneliness. Why did God allow the "wilderness" living Job experienced?

"I have heard of You by the hearing of the ear; But now my eye sees You."

Job 42:5

Read Job 42:5 and rewrite it in your own words.

Job's words give us a peek at the purpose behind all wilderness journeys. After experiencing great personal pain, Job said that his relationship with the Lord went from one based on hearsay to one grounded in experience.

The glory of a personal experience with God far outweighed the drudgery of life's weary circumstances. One commentary notes, "He had known about God, but the pain of his suffering and the folly of his [verbal] challenge [to the Lord] provided the context into which God brought a revelation that opened up for Job a deeper and more personal experience with God."[2]

"I had heard of you but now I've seen you."

Doesn't that summarize what we are all after? Having God in our sight?

Describe a situation in which you "saw" God because of a wilderness experience.

You and I must boldly ask the Lord to let us see Him, even if the light of His presence is best seen against the veil of darkness. We can trust that God loves us enough to allow into our lives only those things necessary to position us for an experiential, abundant relationship with Him. Don't be afraid. Psalm 145:17 states, "The Lord is righteous in all His ways and kind in all His deeds." No matter where He takes us, our greater good is on His heart.

Do you fear what it might take for you to "see" God in your life? If so, take these fears to the Lord in prayer, relinquish control to Him, and ask Him to remind you of His great love for you.

Day 2
Passion and Purpose

So here we are on the edge of the dry and dusty. We're seated Indian style with our elbows on our knees at Etham, shaking our heads because we can't believe that God would choose this road for us. Every now and then we are tempted to look back. To the west of us, we can still catch a faint aroma of the onion, garlic, and fish we'd come to love so much. To the north lays a route that seems much easier than the one God has started us on, but we've made up our minds. If Yahweh was great enough to get Pharaoh to release us, then surely He must know what He's doing. We believe it, but from the looks of things, this isn't going to be a walk in the park. We have to admit, we've got questions. We're wondering why God would choose this.

OUR QUESTIONS AND GOD'S ANSWERS

Believer, you're not the only one asking that question.

Elizabeth asked it: *"My marriage is a mess. My husband has admitted his affair and that he never has any intention of leaving it. I can't believe it. This is not the way things were supposed to turn out. We've been married for 28 years and have four children. You never could have told me that I'd walk a road like this one."*

37

Meagan asked it: *"I want a baby more than anything. When I am around mothers, I get so jealous that I want to cry. Sometimes I do. I excuse myself, go to the bathroom, and tears pour down my face. The doctors have said there's no hope."*

Steve asked it: *"I have a family to provide for. Why they gave me a pink slip, I will never fully understand. I was a valuable commodity at that company, and now it's been a whole year since I lost my job. There is just no work available. I don't know how much longer I can take feeling so inadequate as a father and husband."*

Pamela asked it: *"Why did this have to happen to me? I don't want to be in this wheelchair. How does God expect me to function when my legs don't work? If I'd been born this way, maybe I'd feel differently. But after being mobile 31 years, this is almost too much for me to bear."*

In the margin, write your questions to God. Consider your difficult circumstance or that of a believing friend. Remember, it's OK to ask God "why?" *As long as we are patient*

I've had moments of asking God why too. A couple of years into our marriage I was shocked but excited to discover I was pregnant. Jerry and I celebrated, and the next day we traveled to Chicago where I was to minister at a local church. Right before I was to speak, I went to the restroom and discovered the evidence of trouble. Jerry and I called the doctor and set up an appointment for the next day. The ultrasound revealed what we knew: Our first child had miscarried.

We were devastated.

I'm so glad that God doesn't mind our questions. Just because we wonder aloud does not necessarily mean we don't believe in God's love for us. Habakkuk wondered how long God would allow his crying to continue (Hab. 1:2). Job wondered why God seemed so distant (Job 6:8). Jonah wanted to know why God would send him to the evil city of Nineveh (Jonah 4:2). Even Mary, the mother of Jesus voiced concern when an angel told her she was to bear the Christ, asking, "How can this be?" (Luke 1:34).

Thankfully, God always listens to our questions, even though sometimes He doesn't respond to them in the way we'd like. Instead, He cups our faces tenderly in His hands and whispers, "Follow Me." We must never allow our questions to overshadow the fact that God has all the answers.

Brainstorm other Scripture examples in which people asked God questions about their life circumstances.

GOD'S PASSION FOR OUR PURPOSE

Likely the children of Israel puzzled over God's route for their journey.
Convenience, simplicity, or even happiness weren't God's concerns for the
Hebrews. He wanted their allegiance, their loyalty in the face of difficulty,
and their thoughts focused not on the big threatening enemy but on Him as
Provider and Protector.

> **Do you remember from yesterday why God chose not
> to lead the children of Israel northward east to Canaan?
> Check Exodus 13:17 if you need help recalling why.**

> **On the map in the back put an X over the problem area
> described by God in verse 17.**

God's main purpose was not to get them to Canaan quickly. He knew the
plains of Philistia were filled with enemies prepared to wage war. Not only
was this a consideration in His choice, but God knew Northern Sinai was a
militarized zone. Egypt's army had a very strong presence as well.[3]

Repeatedly in Exodus God said: "Let My people go, that they may serve
Me" (8:1; 9:1). Freedom from Pharaoh was to set the people's hearts on the
complete service and worship of God. He called them out of Egypt and into
Canaan not to achieve military victories but to achieve intimacy with Him.

The Lord desired a people set on forming a close, ongoing, fulfilling relationship with Him—for the Israelites to desire Him over Canaan. The Israelites'
triumphant entrance into a place of milk and honey wasn't to trump the aim of
oneness with the Father.

I struggle with keeping my purpose the same as God's purpose for me.
Sometimes intimacy seems so sedentary, doesn't it? I'm a gal who likes to
get up and do something. Often, I must deliberately refocus my goals back on
God's and remember that winning victories, even worthwhile victories, should
never replace my desire for one-on-one connection with Him. Psalm 27:4 says,
"One thing I ask of the LORD, this is what I seek: that I may dwell in the house
of the LORD all the days of my life, to gaze upon the beauty of the LORD and to
seek him in his temple" (NIV). I want this to be true of me.

> **Rate how well you think you manage to align your
> purposes with God.**

| I'm doing a good job. | Some days I do better than others. | I miss it most of the time. |

"Now when Pharaoh had let the people go, God did not lead them by the way of the land of the Philistines, even though it was near; for God said, 'The people might change their minds when they see war, and return to Egypt.'"
Exodus 13:17

How does God's desire for communion manifest itself in your life?

Why do you think prioritizing intimacy with God can be difficult for today's Christian? What can you do to purposefully counteract these issues?

ARMED FOR THE WRONG BATTLE

"The mind of man plans his way, But the LORD directs his steps."
Proverbs 16:9

Have you ever winced to see someone, who thinks she's prepared, charge into a situation she's obviously not ready to handle? Some people seem so together on the surface, but they lack the maturity and experience for heavy responsibility or opposition. This is like what happened during the exodus.

According to Exodus 13:18, God's people left Egypt "equipped for battle" (ESV). The root word used in the passage is a derivative of the Hebrew word *Khamesh,* which means *five.* God's people left in a formation composed of five divisions: a forward, center, two wings, and a rear guard.[4] They apparently assumed that opposition was imminent and prepared themselves accordingly. This is important because it shows that the very thing they felt prepared to handle—brutal military combat in the desert—was that from which God intended to shield them.

The Lord knew His people were not ready to do any fighting. Though they appeared fully equipped and ready for battle, God wasn't fooled by outward appearances. He wisely recognized that they needed more spiritual preparation to handle the enemies they'd face soon enough.

In the margin describe a situation in which you thought you were ready to handle something you now realize you weren't. In retrospect, did you sense God calling you to follow Him in a different direction at that time?

We must synchronize our primary purposes with God's. No matter how well-prepared we think we are, we must realize that we can neither accomplish abundant life with God nor overcome the Enemy's advances without the Lord's help. While we often want the easiest and least challenging route to abundant life in Christ, we must acknowledge that God wants to take us on the path that fosters a deeper relationship with Him. He wants us to lay aside our determination to do life our way and follow Him. Only when we do this can we truly become ready to face what lies ahead.

Check your life. What is your primary aim?

- I want to win battles and be a spiritual champion so I can wave the flag of success before others.
- I want to enjoy the fruits of "milk and honey" now even if intimacy with God is not flourishing.
- I want to feast on milk and honey in the knowledge that I can do so because I've gained strength and power through intimacy with God.

Day 3
The $500 Story

Five hundred dollars. That's the centerpiece of this story. When my sister and I were toddlers, my parents lived in a makeshift apartment in a bad part of town. One day when Mom reached for a can of beans once again the only food in our home—she burst into tears of frustration. My father came home to find her crying a river; she was tired of our scant existence.

Dad was in seminary. My mother felt awful for the way she felt about the life he was able to provide. Mom said, "Honey, if God would just give us $500 to get through the month, just enough to get some food in the house and to take care of a couple of other necessities, I could keep going." My father replied, "If God doesn't answer your cry, I'll quit school and get a full-time job."

They prayed. God heard.

Dad went to school the next day and opened his on-campus mailbox. Inside rested a $500 money order.

This incident happened over 40 years ago. Today my parents remember it as a sign of God's hand on their lives during a wilderness experience. The story serves as a reminder of God's faithfulness. It encourages them to rely on God in the good times and the rough, resting in the knowledge that God is always in control. In the midst of the dry and dusty wilderness of their lives, God gave them a $500 story to be a reminder of His love and continued protection of their family—even and especially when times got tough.

Recall a time in your wilderness when God gave you a $500 story. Prepare to share this experience with your group this week.

RALLYING TO REMEMBER

In the Book of Deuteronomy Moses rallied the people to remember where they'd been and what they'd faced with God. He wanted them to have a $500 story of their own. When the Hebrews were perched on the edge of the promised land, Moses recounted for them the various highlights of their 40-year journey through the desert.

> *"He humbled you and let you be hungry, and fed you with manna which you did not know, nor did your fathers know, that He might make you understand that man does not live by bread alone, but man lives by everything that proceeds out of the mouth of the LORD. Your clothing did not wear out on you, nor did your foot swell these forty years."*
>
> Deuteronomy 8:3-4

Using the New American Standard Bible (in the margin), fill in the blanks from Deuteronomy 8:3-4:

"He _____ you and let you be _____, and fed you with manna which you did not know, nor did your fathers know, that He might make you _____ that man does not live by bread alone, but man lives by everything that proceeds out of the _____ of the _____.

Your _____ did not wear out on you, nor did your _____ swell these _____ years."

Which portion of these verses stands out to you the most and why?

In this passage Moses pointed out things the Israelites ought to deliberately recall. He wanted them to recognize that God should remain their primary focus and hearts' desire as they approached the beauties and glories of Canaan. Moses encouraged them not to forget that God was the source of all good things.

What change might remembering God's goodness bring about in your attitude when you are in the wilderness? in the land of abundance?

Turn to your map. Find and circle Kadesh-barnea, on the southern edge of Canaan.

According to Deuteronomy 1:2, how long should the journey from their last location, Horeb (Mount Sinai), have taken?

▨ 11 days   ▨ 18 months   ▨ 111 years

"It is eleven days' journey from Horeb by the way of Mount Seir to Kadesh-barnea."
Deuteronomy 1:2

For four decades the Israelites traveled circles in this patch of land that was only steps away from their destiny. The key to taking full possession of the land God promised was obedience, but the key to finding full appreciation of it was found in remembering God's goodness and protection through their extended years in the wilderness. By asking the people to remember their trek with the Lord, Moses encouraged the Israelites to value their wilderness experience.

Remembering good stuff takes effort, doesn't it? Remembering and retelling a $500 story when you've only got a penny in your pocket takes discipline. Purposefully turning our attention onto what God is doing in the midst of the driest seasons of our lives requires us to zero in on God's goodness to us in the midst of our journeys.

What are some practical ways that you remember God's goodness in lean times?

Consider starting a "$500 story journal." This can be a file on your computer or a simple spiral notebook. It is not a diary of random daily ocurrances but a record of God's hand in your life. This will serve as a catalyst for you and your family to remember God's goodness for years to come.

Which of the following best describes your current stop on the wilderness journey?

▨ I'm in Egypt still contemplating freedom.
▨ I'm at Etham on the edge of the wilderness. I'm just getting started.
▨ I'm wandering in a desert, so I must be in the middle of my journey.
▨ I'm at Kadesh-barnea. I'm at the edge of an abundant relationship with God!

Plan to describe to your group where you are in your walk with God.

On the left side of this chart, list the toughest parts of your personal wilderness journey right now. On the right side, list evidences of God's hand in the midst of it.

PREPARING FOR THE TEST

Read Deuteronomy 8:2 in which Moses prepared the people for their entry into Canaan.

God's allowance of the difficulties of the wilderness was to prepare the Israelites by doing two things: testing their intentions and calling them to obedience. He did this by allowing the wilderness to humble them.

In the preceding paragraph, circle the two things God wanted to do before the Hebrews entered Canaan. Underline the means through which He would accomplish this.

The Lord used the Israelites' time in the desert to strip from them any pride that might keep them from blossoming into the submissive, teachable people He desired. Each of us can think of people who, after beginning to see God's goodness in their lives, began to think more highly of themselves than they ought. The wilderness, designed to foster humility, presented hardships that revealed the hidden motives and objectives of their hearts.

Do you remember the children's movie and Broadway play *Annie*? We were all captivated by the bouncy little redhead who needed a family to love her. In the end, all works out for her good, just like any good Disney movie should—but the good ending doesn't come without difficulty. A couple posing as her parents show up to claim her when a reward is offered. As they drive away with Annie and the money, their true intentions are quickly revealed. They are immediately disgusted and frustrated with the demands of parenting when Annie needs to stop and "go to the potty." They are trying to get out of town, and this little girl is in the way. The most simple interruption to their plan reveals the intent of their heart.

The wilderness is designed to reveal whether we really want God or if we just want to "get out of town" and to Canaan as soon as possible. He is interested in knowing if we've submitted to the wilderness only to receive the rewards that come with Canaan or if we truly desire Him more than anything … even the rewards.

What have the frustrations and interruptions of the wilderness revealed to you about your heart's intentions?

Charles Spurgeon described the wilderness as "the Oxford and Cambridge for God's students. There they went to the University and he taught and trained them, and they took their degree before they entered into the promised land."

The people who left Egypt were humbled not only to purify their hearts' intentions but also to qualify their obedience. Obeying is easy when it makes sense and when milk and honey are flowing all around us, but the true test of our commitment is best seen when there is no refreshment in sight, just plain after plain of dry wasteland. Will we obey God even then?

What have you found is the hardest thing for you to obey God about right now?

Right now, call a friend. Ask her to give you an evaluation of your walk with God as she sees it in these three areas.

1. **Are you a humble person who appreciates God's goodness to you? during dry seasons? during abundant seasons?**
2. **Do you say or do anything that calls into question your motives for following God?**
3. **Does it appear that your primary aim is to obey God at all costs?**

Share with her where you are struggling in each of these areas, and then ask her to pray with you and to keep you accountable.

Day 4
Covered by Cloud & Led By Fire

For three days we've discussed the wilderness and looked into reasons why God allows it in the lives of His people. We found that God brought the Israelites to the wilderness; they didn't happen on it by mistake. We found that God is not nearly as interested in mapping out the most convenient route for us as He is in cementing and growing our relationship with Him. Yesterday we saw that remembering God's hand in our lives during the lean times helps us better appreciate the bounty of the great times. The wilderness fosters humility and strengthens our commitment to obedience.

Now that we have some clarity on why God allows wilderness times, I want to shift our thinking to another line of questioning: How? How, for instance, does God expect us to make it to Canaan in circumstances like those we face? How are we supposed to support a passion regarding our purpose and keep a sense of enthusiasm about our journeys when our morale is low? When tired of walking mile after long hot mile, how can we keep our minds focused on our destination? Let's turn our attention back to Exodus 13.

"The Lord was going before them in a pillar of cloud by day to lead them on the way, and in a pillar of fire by night to give them light, that they might travel by day and by night. He did not take away the pillar of cloud by day, nor the pillar of fire by night, from before the people."
Exodus 13:21-22

Read Exodus 13:21-22. How did God manifest Himself during the day? at night?

God was there & it was unstentanous

What purpose did these manifestations serve?

When did God withhold the manifestations?

From the moment the Israelites set camp at Etham, God miraculously revealed His presence. He literally assumed a visible form. Suddenly the people did not have to rely on faith that God was with them; they could see Him for themselves. He revealed His glory, shrouded by a cloud and a fire, to mere men. In His grace and love for His feeble children, the Lord showed His presence so that they could be certain He was with them on the journey. Even during the darkest hours they could catch a glimpse of God's presence.

On the map draw a cloud and fire at Etham to indicate the place where God evidenced His presence.

Some scholars suggest all sorts of attempted explanations of what the Israelites really saw: bad weather, haze, or even a dust kicked up as the Israelites walked are among the favored options. Yet nothing explains the fact that God remained before the people in the form of a cloud by day and a fire at night for 40 years. (Even the worst weather doesn't last that long!) The cloud and fire were supernatural. They were physical pictures of God's guiding presence. They provided tangible evidence that the Israelites were not alone.

Do you believe God desires to reveal Himself to modern-day believers? In the margin respond why or why not.

The term *theophany* refers to God taking on a finite form to directly reveal His presence and activity to man. Since Christ came to earth in human form, theophanies are no longer necessary (see Heb. 1:1-2). In Old Testament times, however, a theophany provided a remarkable indicator of God's interest in and support for His people. Other theophanies appear in passages such as Genesis 16:7-13 and 2 Chronicles 5:11-14.

God still chooses to display Himself to people today when, for reasons we'll never know, He orchestrates nature or circumstances to dramatically show His presence. Although manifesting Himself directly is no longer God's way of relating to His people as it was during the wilderness wanderings, His desire has not changed. He still wants to make Himself fully known to us and does so by working through what He has created. He can and will encourage us in our journey by allowing, when He sees fit, His children to have visible evidence of His working on our behalf. Although theophanies were specifically for Old Testament believers, we still have the privilege of experiencing God's manifest presence and expecting miracles in our lives.

See the definition of God's manifest presence in the margin. How does God's revelation of Himself to Israel differ from how He reveals Himself to us today?

Through the Holy Spirit

GOD REVEALED

I just got off of the phone with Shana, a long-time friend. She's a delightful woman in the midst of a five-year journey through the wilderness. Her life took a downward spiral after the death of her beloved husband. When he passed, she was ostracized by the church family in which they had served.

> **Theophany—** A theological term used to describe a God-appearance when God assumes a form and supernaturally shows Himself within the natural realm.

> God's manifest presence is His clear, obvious, visible, revealed, presence in your life.

Finally, she moved to another state where she's felt nothing but loneliness and depression. Her search for a fulfilling job has left her empty-handed. In every area of her life, she runs into walls. Her depression has led to shocking decisions and the heart-wrenching plea: "I just feel so alone. Does God remember me at all? I need to know that He is still here." What Shana desires is a manifestation of God's presence. She feels desperate and desires that God make Himself known in an unmistakable way.

In the midst of the wilderness, what she wants—what we all want—is a cloud—a visible display of God's presence and power with her. Wouldn't it be nice for God to come down and linger over the person we are to marry or the building where our new job awaits? Wouldn't it be great to know for sure this house was the one we should put an offer on because God's cloud hung just over the roof line?

Seeing God's presence would encourage us by giving us confirmation He was still with us. As it turns out, not only do we think it'd be a good idea to have this kind of sure leading through life but so does God! The same desire God had to manifest Himself to the children of Israel centuries ago remains. In fact, He now uses what He considers a more suitable, effective, and constant way to reveal Himself to all of His children at any time and in any place. While theophanies were temporary, His current means of manifestation is constant.

Turn to John 14:16-17. How does God manifest Himself to us today?

Today the power and presence of the Holy Spirit helps us come to the knowledge and understanding of God's revealed truth. That same Spirit comforts us, encouraging us daily that God is indeed with us.

Draw a line connecting the verses that show similarities between the Holy Spirit and ancient Israel's cloud.

John 16:13   Exodus 13:22—ever present
John 16:14   Exodus 13:21—a Guide
Psalm 139:7-10   Exodus 14:19—Revealer of Truth

FROM THE SPIRITUAL TO THE PHYSICAL

While I celebrate the Holy Spirit's presence in our lives, I want to challenge you to consider that God might want to minister to you in a miraculous way that you can experience through one of your five senses. I've always known theologically that God can still reveal Himself in the natural realm in a visible way but never thought it was possible in my life. I've spent years in self-imposed cozy Christian comfort zones where it was safer not to expect much out of God. The cloud and fire allowed Israel to experience God in ways they never had before.

We must be open for Him to do the same for us. I believe He wants you to see Him work in ways that your eyes have not yet beheld and your mind has not yet conceived that are consistent with His holy character as revealed in Scripture. Once you begin to expect Him and see Him in this way, you'll never be the same again. You'll be ruined for mere religion forever.

Have you ever experienced a clear manifestation of God's presence in your life?

☐ yes ☐ not sure ☐ never

If yes, explain the miracle and prepare to share it with your group.

Do you expectantly believe that miracles are still possible?

☐ yes ☐ not sure ☐ not at all

According to Romans 1:20 and Psalm 19:1-4 every human has opportunity to see God manifesting Himself every day.

"By taking a long and thoughtful look at what God has created, people have always been able to see what their eyes as such can't see: eternal power, for instance, and the mystery of his divine being. So nobody has a good excuse [for not believing]" (Rom. 1:20, MSG).

"The heavens proclaim the glory of God. The skies display his craftsmanship. Day after day they continue to speak; night after night they make him known. They speak without a sound or word; their voice is never heard. Yet their message has gone throughout the earth, and their words to all the world" (Ps. 19:1-4, NLT).

I pray that the Holy Spirit will open your eyes so that you can see Him moving in your life in unusual ways. Have you ever considered that God can cause a phone call to come, an e-mail to be sent, a job to be offered, a financial gift to arrive, your husband to be softened, an addiction to end, a tumor to disappear, or a person to speak a word in due season that will manifest His presence and activity supernaturally in your life?

May you never doubt that God is with you on the journey, guiding your every step. The Holy Spirit is calling you, dear friend, to see Him in the real world and in real time. Is your heart burning? Mine is, because I've seen God show up enough now to never question the possibility again. If you dare, ask God to open your eyes to see Him and then be on the lookout for His manifest presence and supernatural activity in your life.

Expect God's presence to overshadow you!

Day 5
Refreshed by a River

It was a tough day. I woke up late, so having a quiet time or getting in a little exercise were out of the question. Jerry hadn't said "good morning" before going out for coffee. I took a shower. It was cold. Both boys woke up cranky. I asked them what they wanted for breakfast. Eggs. I opened the fridge; no eggs. Frustrated, I pulled out the pancake batter and put some in the mixing bowl only to remember: no eggs. On top of that, there was about an eighth of a teaspoon of milk in the gallon jug in the fridge. (I'm going to kill whoever put that back in there.) Cereal? No milk! URGH!

Throughout the day we were late for every appointment and each line was longer than the last. By the time we made it home, we were beat and my attitude was sour. I threw the keys on the table, plopped my purse on the floor, sent the little ones up to their room for some quiet time, and headed down the hall to hide from the day.

That's when I saw it: a huge bouquet of the most beautiful flowers I'd ever seen waited on my night stand. Attached was a note from Jerry, simply saying, "Just because."

A little refreshment right in the nick of time.

OASIS IN THE WILDERNESS

Israel's journey was rough. They left Egypt and camped at Etham, narrowly escaped impending death at the hands of the Egyptians, and soon found themselves so thirsty that their mouths ached. Not surprisingly, they began complaining to their leader and wishing for relief. Then, seemingly out of nowhere, a heavenly gift arrived "just because."

> **Put yourself in the Israelites' sandals in Exodus 15. Which of the following best describes your attitude toward the bounty offered in verse 27?**
> ▢ Well, it's about time!
> ▢ Water? Fresh fruit? Praise God!
> ▢ Why go any farther? Let's stop here.
> ▢ I was hoping for more.

God provided an oasis at the Israelites' second stopping place after crossing the Red Sea. There they were delighted to discover refreshment and shade for themselves and their livestock. Elim was "the most extensive watercourse in the western desert—an oasis, adorned with a great variety of trees, among which the palm is still conspicuous, and fertilized by a copious stream. It is estimated to be a mile in breadth."[6] Imagine the discouraged and parched Hebrews peering through the blurry haze covering the sand to discover the welcoming cover of palm trees— not just 1 but 70! Sheer joy must have spread through the Israelites.

> **Turn to your map and find Elim. Draw a glass or a drop of water at Elim to remind you of the refreshment Israel found.**

> **Israel consisted of 12 tribes. Why might the number of wells at Elim be significant (v. 27)?**

God gave the weary, thirsty Hebrews exactly what they needed to suit their precise circumstances. Surely the 12 springs served as a great illustration of God's overwhelming care and very specific concern for their needs. God knows exactly what's needed to refresh you too. He knows what is required to refuel your tank and to encourage you in your journey.

> **In what specific areas do you need refreshment right now? Brainstorm a list of ways the Lord might choose to provide it. Don't be afraid to dream big, but remember God is sovereign and knows what's best for you.**

"Then they came to Elim where there were twelve springs of water and seventy date palms, and they camped there beside the waters."
Exodus 15:27

"I will open rivers on the bare heights, and fountains in the midst of the valleys. I will make the wilderness a pool of water, and the dry land springs of water."
Isaiah 41:18, ESV

Jerry and I have friends who pastor a church that is a healing place of shelter for those hurt by years of hardship and spiritual discouragement. Under the eaves of that church people find refreshment and renewal in their relationships with the Lord. For years this fellowship has provided the encouragement that their community needs. Elim was Israel's healing place. It was a divinely appointed opportunity for the children of Israel to regroup, refocus, and prepare to continue the journey.

How can we make it successfully through our dry and dusty journey? We are covered by a cloud of God's presence as we learned yesterday and we must also keep in mind that God will refresh us by a river of His provision. He will provide healing places and oases for us too. We will not always be engulfed with fatigue as we travel from one day to the next. Instead, our Father will remain mindful of us, knowing our needs and caring for us in the midst of our journeys.

Has the Lord ever provided a healing place for you? If so, what did it look like?

Reminding ourselves of God's love for us in the wilderness is always of utmost importance. Pray the following three verses aloud to God just as I have written them. Consider copying them on an index card to keep with you for encouragement when things get tough.

God:
According to Philippians 4:19 I believe that You will meet all of my needs according to Your glorious riches in Christ Jesus. Lord, thank You that You are a shield around me. You are my glory and the lifter of my head (Ps. 3:3). As I journey, Lord, please reveal Your love for me that, according to Ephesians 3:17-20, surpasses knowledge and fills life with Your fullness. Thank You for being able to do immeasurably more than I can ask.
In Jesus' name I pray, Amen.

Elim was not a small oasis; it held an overwhelmingly enormous supply of underground water capable of sustaining millions. Sister, keep marching forward in full assurance that the Lord will abundantly supply every one of your needs (see Phil. 4:19).

WASTELAND REFRESHMENT

While a desert and a wilderness may appear similar, a closer look reveals a huge difference. A wilderness is peppered with oases, places of hope for a weary traveler. A desert is a barren expanse that can support little life or vegetation. A wilderness can support a large variety of animal life. At first it seems that the wilderness through which God led His people was a desert, but in reality it was a place with grassy areas, upland plains, and even surface water. God's people were able to withstand the journey because God led them not through an arid desert but into a wilderness complete with natural rest stops.

Meditate on the following verses, and record anything the Holy Spirit reveals to you about each one.
Psalm 23:2-3

1 Corinthians 10:13

In the margin write other passages that comfort you in tough times. Share these with your group this week.

Sister, I know the journey might be tough, but please remember that God leads us not to deserts but through wildernesses. His wildernesses. Moreover, the Lord strategically places "Elims" in our paths that will refresh us when we think we can stand no more. Your wilderness is purposefully and sovereignly spotted with oasis after oasis, grassy knoll after grassy knoll, at just the right time to provide you the nourishment you need.

Keep your head up and feet moving forward as you travel on your life's journey. God loves you and has not forgotten you. You left Egypt under the guidance of Jehovah God, and He will never lead you into a place that will not work toward accomplishing His purposes for you.

You have an ever-flowing, overabundant supply of "flow[ing] rivers of living water" within you (John 7:38). This supply is the Holy Spirit empowering you, comforting you, and encouraging you to press on.

1. Leon J. Wood. *A Survey of Israel's History* (Grand Rapids, MI: Zondervan, 1986), 109.
2. Robert B. Hughes et. al. *Tyndale Concise Bible Commentary* (Wheaton, IL: Tyndale House, 2001), 197.
3. Philip Graham Ryken. *Exodus: Saved for God's Glory* (Wheaton, IL: Crossway Books, 2005), 380.
4. H.D.M. Spence-Jones, *The Pulpit Commentary: Exodus,* Volume 1 (Bellingham, WA: Logos Research Systems, 2004), 306.
5. Ryken, 419.
6. Robert Jamieson et. al. *A Commentary, Critical and Explanatory on the Old and New Testaments* (Oak Harbor, WA: Logos Research Systems, 1997), Ex. 15:27.

Session 3
Viewer Guide

God is predictable in His _character_ but He is completely unpredictable in His _activity_.
God is always moving

We have to let God be God when it comes to how He wants to _govern_ our lives.

Your victory is _guaranteed_ in Scripture.

Moses said four things:

Be _fearless_.

Be _still_.

Be _watchful_.

Be _silent_.

Psalms 145:17-18
my God is kind

The same God who worked on our behalf _yesterday_ is the same God who can work on our behalf _today_.

fear causes to forget

Stand. Psalm 46:10
don't set so you
give no keep on
God

When you are in the wilderness

Psalm 46:10
"Cease striving and know that I am God; I will be exalted among the nations, I will be exalted in the earth."

Standing and stillness are _prerequisites_ for watchfulness.

Abundant life, promised land living is not for _tomorrow_ —it is for today—watch for it.

col 4:18

Train yourself to be quiet. Train yourself not to open your mouth in arrogance or complaining.

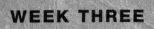

EXPERIENCING GOD

I shared my heart with a spiritual mentor. Jerry and I had been married for three years and our relationship lay in shambles. We couldn't talk without arguing. We pushed one another out as I began to neglect his needs, becoming more concerned with my friends, my life, and my needs than with his. He responded in kind. The situation felt impossible.

My mentor listened to my complaints on and off for 18 months, but this time she stopped listening and started speaking. Her words carried the authority of God: "Priscilla, I believe in miracles. I am certain that one of the reasons for the wilderness seasons of our lives is so that we'll start expecting more out of God than ever before. Stop complaining and start asking for and anticipating God's supernatural activity. Expect the unexpected. He can fix this marriage. Ask Him. Let Him."

The Lord could and did fix our marriage. While at the time I believed that neither Jerry nor I could rediscover a friendly and passionate relationship with one another, the Lord knew better. God can work out every "impossible" situation for His glory.

Day 1
Expecting the Unexpected

Why does God allow the wilderness? That's the question this week. Each time I encounter a spiritual desert, I'm learning to remind myself that every wilderness season increases my chances to see God's supernatural and miraculous power working for my good. When I get bogged down by difficult times, I now expect the Lord to do something unexpected to either free me from my situation or help me to deal with it. Either way, I find that He raises my level of awe regarding His ability.

Which describes your response to the margin statement?
- **I believe it and look forward to seeing God's miracles.**
- **I'm not sure I believe that. You'll have to convince me.**
- **Why should I have to suffer to better see God?**

How might difficulty sharpen our focus on God's intervention in our lives?

Every wilderness season increases the likelihood that [we'll] see God's supernatural and miraculous power working for [our] good.

A miracle is a divine supernatural occurrence in which God overrules the natural order of earth to reveal His presence and power. "It is an occurrence at once above nature and above man. It shows the intervention of a power that is not limited by the laws either of matter or of mind, a power interrupting the fixed laws which govern their movements, a supernatural power."[1]

In the margin write your own definition of a miracle.

Which more nearly fits what you believe?
- ▨ God only did miracles in the Bible.
- ▨ Miracles are only for other people.
- ▨ I can really experience a miracle in my life.
- ▨ If God has done a miracle for me, I'm unaware of it.
- ▨ God doesn't care about me, so I don't want to set myself up for more disappointment.

BETWEEN A ROCK AND A HARD PLACE

Have you ever noticed that God's way often leads between two brick walls? Sometimes living according to His plans can seem uncomfortable, even impossible. Such was the case for several biblical figures.

NOAH built an ark when there was no rain.
ESTHER stood before a king with an outlandish request.
DANIEL was in a lion's den with no obvious protection.
DAVID ran for his life from an angry, jealous king.
MARY and MARTHA's sick brother died.
PAUL and SILAS were trapped in prison at the midnight hour.

In each situation, hope seemed futile. Yet God used every one of these circumstances to bring Himself glory while allowing the participants a miraculous glimpse of His awesome power. If you can't figure out how to navigate the path before you, take heart. When you can't imagine that divine intervention is at your doorstep, get ready. Doing life God's way, especially when times seem difficult, often includes miraculous surprises.

Choose two of the following biblical examples, then answer the questions in regard to your selection.
- • Hagar's story (Gen. 21:9-20)
- • The story of Elisha and his servant (2 Kings 6:8-23)
- • Jonah's story (Jonah 1:17–2:10)

What difficult circumstances did the Lord allow and what response did this elicit from the parties involved?

How did the Lord show Himself strong in the situation?

What important lessons did those in the stories learn about themselves? about God's faithfulness and power?

How does this example encourage you?

"Tell the sons of Israel to turn back and camp before Pi-hahiroth, between Migdol and the sea; you shall camp in front of Baal-zephon, opposite it, by the sea."
Exodus 14:2

When Hagar, Elisha and his servant, and Jonah stared down the barrel of disaster, God showed Himself as a hero. The Hebrews learned to see the Lord in a similar light. When the children of Israel left Etham, God gave Moses specific instructions regarding the direction His people were to take.

Circle the words *turn back* in Exodus 14:2. Look at your map. Considering Migdol's location in relation to Etham and Canaan, what's your opinion of God's direction?

Recall a time when you felt like the directions God gave seemed to go the opposite way you were headed. In the margin describe how it felt.

In the early days of their desert trek, Israel held a low opinion of God's decisions. When He led them to the beach at the Red Sea, most were so against the idea that they whined, "Is it because there were no graves in Egypt that you have taken us away to die in the wilderness? Why have you dealt with us in this way, bringing us out of Egypt? … For it would have been better for us to serve the Egyptians than to die in the wilderness" (Ex. 14:11-12). These cynical comments were hugely sarcastic. One commentator noted, "The phrase 'no graves in Egypt' borders on the humorous because Egypt was the land of graves, death, and preoccupation with the afterlife."[2]

As the Israelites looked at the impassable body of water before them and the line of advancing Egyptian chariots behind, they felt certain that God and Moses had surely made a mistake in leading them toward the Red Sea. Audaciously, though perhaps out of fear, the Israelites taunted their leader. In doing so, they questioned the Lord's guidance.

How often do you question the Lord's guidance?

never   seldom   sometimes   often

Explain in the margin what questioning God reveals about our estimation of His ability to make decisions.

We often respond to "Red Sea" circumstances like they did. When we see that following God includes challenges, we start to question His authority. Worse yet, we long for the very thing from which Christ freed us. The memory of the brutality of slavery fades. The idea of relying on a God we can't see makes us feel out-of-control and weak. If we don't take care, our lack of faith will cause us to turn from the source of our salvation.

The Lord is leading a friend of mine on a journey into a deeper relationship with Him. She's noticed that as her husband sees changes in her prayer life, friends, expectations, and faith in God, he becomes increasingly callous and defensive. The tension in her marriage tempts her to resettle in a life of spiritual complacency. I can relate. When my marriage took a difficult turn in the early years, I responded to my husband and to God with frustration. Like the children of Israel, I allowed my "Red Sea" circumstance to turn my eyes to the seeming ease I'd left behind in my life as a single. I started questioning whether God was even capable of working in my life.

What are the dangers of looking back to past experiences when encountering our own "Red Seas"?

POSITIONED FOR A MIRACLE

Yesterday Jerry and I took the boys to see a Veggie Tales® movie about three normal guys chosen to go back to the 17th century. Unbeknownst to them, they'd been selected as the heroes to save a princess and prince from the evil uncle's plans to overtake their father's throne. The three heroes felt ill-equipped to handle the task. They kept saying, "We are not heroes. You've got the wrong people." Yet time after time they supernaturally overcame problems.

Not until the end of the movie did they realize their steps were guided by a king watching over them. At the end of the movie they came face to face with the true king who rewarded them for saving his children. He explained that every time they faced an impossible situation, he supplied them with the miraculous means to overcome. They realized that their steps were guided by a king who watched their every move and equipped them for the journey.

The Lord specifically chose the Israelites for the wilderness journey. Their meeting with the Red Sea was not a mistake. In fact, the entire dry and dusty journey was God's plan. He gave them specific directions that led them there. When He took the people between a rock—Pharaoh's army—and a hard place—the Red Sea—He positioned them for a miracle. He wants to accomplish similar things in our lives.

In what way would you describe your life now as being in a Red Sea circumstance? Do you expect that God can do a miracle with your circumstance?

"Was it not You who dried up the sea, The waters of the great deep; Who made the depths of the sea a pathway for the redeemed to cross over?"
Isaiah 51:10

Read Exodus 14:13-31. On your map, put a "1" at the Red Sea crossing to mark God's first wilderness miracle.

At the beginning of their long, weary march through the wilderness, God wanted the people to see and experience a personal manifestation of His ability. He wanted them reliant on a miraculous move only He could pull off. Seeing God's power in action at the Red Sea would not only foster their belief and confidence in God but would serve as a bedrock remembrance of His powerful faithfulness for centuries to come.

When God allows you to face a "Red Sea," don't become discouraged. Don't whine and question the Lord's ability. Expect that God is positioning you to see Him work in your life in a unique and unusual way.

Record the details of a personal miracle. How did it impact your level of faith and encourage your commitment to follow God? Repeat the exercise for a miracle you've witnessed in the life of another.

	The Miracle	The Impact	The Commitment
Your life			
Another's life			

Let your "Red Sea" circumstances foster enthusiasm and anticipation about the God-intervention planned for you. Expect the unexpected! God leads us to places where His power shows up in new and astonishing ways. May an awesome display of His power strengthen your faith.

Day 2
A Sweeter Journey

Jerry and I stock extra bottled water on a shelf in the garage. This week I decided to bring a whole case into the kitchen. As I hoisted a case off the high garage shelf, the weight of 20 liters settled into my arms. My back and knees tensed in pain, and I almost dropped the entire case. I never expected water to be so heavy!

The Hebrew multitude needed immense provision to survive. On the heels of the victory at the Red Sea, Israel celebrated and sang praises to God (Ex. 15). God's miracle on their behalf fired their confidence in Him. Surely, they reasoned, we'll face smooth sailing now. But as they took an eastward turn into the Wilderness of Shur, some of their supplies began to wane. Not surprisingly, they could not pack and carry enough water to sustain them.

How should the miracle at the Red Sea have affected Israel's attitude about their need for water?

"When they came to Marah, they could not drink the waters of Marah, for they were bitter; therefore it was named Marah."

Exodus 15:23

The Hebrews journeyed three long, hot days from the Red Sea into the Wilderness of Shur. Thirst haunted them. Hope grew when someone spotted a waterhole, but feelings of relief soon gave way to disappointment.

Which best describes the waters at Marah?
■ **refreshing** ■ **muddy** ■ **warm** ☑ **bitter**

The dehydrated multitude thought they'd found a solution to their problem, but a closer look and a taste of the waters revealed that the find would do them no good. Marah's springs weren't fit for human consumption. The waters were brackish and most likely filled with "salt, minerals, or perhaps even poison."[3] The human body can only survive three to five days without water, so imagine the Israelites' disgust, frustration, and panic as they faced the dilemma. Bitterness toward God quickly grew among the multitude of refugees. Why, they questioned, would a good God put undrinkable water before a dehydrated crowd?

Why do you think God allowed the thirsty Israelites to come across undrinkable water? Respond in margin.

MARAH'S MIRAGE

Every wilderness journey has a "Marah," where refreshment and hope seem imminent but fail to deliver. You need this refreshment desperately because like the Israelites you've been without a thirst quencher far too long. Travel under the torrid rays of life has left you hot, tired, and frustrated.

Now your heart skips and a smile etches itself into the corners of your frowned soul because there's a glimmer of hope ahead. Surely now your hot, weary days of thirst are over. What's kept you going through the wilderness was your belief that a cool, refreshing respite was not far out of reach.

- Just around the next corner you'll get the promotion.
- Your spouse will come back physically and emotionally.
- Your boyfriend assures you he will pop the question.
- The doctor has said this will be a cure.
- The lost relationship is on the brink of recovery.
- The fertility treatment will work this time.
- The investment broker says your risk will pay off.

You believe God has sent an answer to finally complete this part of your journey. You run and dive in head first, fully committing yourself because satisfaction is looming. Then at the last minute you're overlooked for the promotion, divorce papers appear at your door, you're in the one percent of people for whom the medication won't be effective, the stock crashes, the relationship crumbles, the boyfriend calls it quits. Marah's waters had only been a mirage of fulfillment that didn't satisfy like you thought they would.

Through what difficult wilderness have you trudged with high hopes that the answer was coming soon?

Were you ever disappointed when the outcome was not what you expected? Explain.

My friend Crystal is experiencing the bitter waters of Marah. She's a spunky 31-year-old who is smart and articulate. After finishing her master's in business she held high expectations for her new career. With a glowing report from her university and tremendous recommendations from professors and past employers, she ventured into the job market. But when interview after interview turned up no results, her excitement waned.

When a company finally offered Crystal her dream job, she prepared for her new position with a burst of enthusiasm and renewed confidence.

one

*"O God, You
are my God; I
shall seek You
earnestly; My
soul thirsts for
You, my flesh
yearns for You,
In a dry and
weary land
where there is
no water."*
Psalm 63:1

Two nights before she was to start her new job, however, Crystal received a letter. The company had just been bought out by a major affiliate. Her promised position was eliminated, the offer retracted.

Have you ever felt frustrated or angry at God because of a disappointment you have faced? ▪ yes ▪ no

David knew what it was like to be frustrated and disappointed with God. We see a great example in 1 Chronicles 13:2-12.

What was David attempting to do?

What happened to cause David's disappointment?

What emotions did he experience?

*"In You, O LORD,
I have taken
refuge; Let
me never be
ashamed; In
Your righteous-
ness deliver me."*
Psalm 30:1

When God allows circumstances like David faced, we can be certain He has a purpose. Everything He leads us to, even Marah, is for a specific reason. Marahs position us to put our hope not in ourselves or in the world but in God. We can't anticipate and provide for life's trials, but the Lord can and does. The Lord wants us to thirst not after a quick fix to our problems but after the life-altering refreshment of His provision (see Ps. 63:1).

How did God provide for their thirst? (Ex. 15:23-25).

On your map find Marah. Write a number "2" beside it to indicate God's second miracle in the wilderness.

*God's goal for
our journeys is
that we not only
see the miracle
of His deliver-
ance at our Red
Seas but that
we experience
the miracle of
His provision
beyond them.*

In the margin describe how the obvious correlation between the Red Sea miracle and that of Marah ought to have impacted Israel's faith.

SWEET WATER FOR THE WILDERNESS

Often the Lord purposefully allows the nourishment provided by this world to taste like bitter waters to us so that we come to understand the importance of His touch on our circumstances. Without God's influence, nothing in this world can really quench the deep thirst of our souls.

God's goal for our journeys is that we not only see the miracle of His deliverance at our Red Seas but that we experience the miracle of His provision beyond them. When Moses cried out on behalf of the people, the Lord gave a solution. He turned their bitterness into sweetness (Ex. 15:25). This is what God does when we cry out to Him, displaying our vulnerability during seasons of distress and giving Him our need for emotional healing in the face of disappointment. He is the One who can turn the bitter into the sweet.

When disappointed is your tendency to:
▣ cry out to God   or   ▣ harbor your frustration

Explain your response.

According to 1 Chronicles 5:20 and 2 Samuel 22:7, how did God respond to His children's cries?

"To all who mourn in Israel, he will give a crown of beauty for ashes, a joyous blessing instead of mourning, festive praise instead of despair. In their righteousness, they will be like great oaks that the Lord has planted for His own glory."
Isaiah 61:3, NLT

Scripture is clear that God hears and responds to the cries of His people. When life's biggest disappointments cause a bitterness that you just can't seem to shake, know that the Lord wants to step in and reveal the miracle of His restoring power in your heart. He can take your biggest struggle and heartache—the one that causes your chest to ache with frustration—and turn it into the sweet spot on which your spiritual outlook hinges.

Meditate on Isaiah 61:3 and ask God to make something sweet out of your bitterness. I promise you He can; and if you trust Him, He will!

Day 3
This Is Only a Test

I've always been intimidated by math. The Lord didn't see fit to connect the number wires in my brain. The first week of my freshman year our professor explained he'd routinely test our knowledge of each week's material. Should a student maintain an "A" average on these quizzes, he or she would earn exemption from the cumulative final. Each week I listened intently to the professor and visited the tutoring lounge often. Every Friday I faced the quiz with confidence because I'd taken the time to carefully review and internalize each lesson. I determined to maintain an "A" because I knew that passing a cumulative exam would be next to impossible for a mathematically-challenged girl like me.

Look up Exodus 15:25; 16:4; and Deuteronomy 8:2. What commonality do these verses share?

"In this you greatly rejoice, even though now for a little while, if neces-sary, you have been distressed by various trials, so that the proof of your faith, being more precious than gold which is perishable, even though tested by fire, may be found to result in praise and glory and honor at the revelation of Jesus Christ."
1 Peter 1:6-7

In each of these instances, the Lord decided to test His people. Every wilder-ness is compiled of one test after another. Each is designed to better reveal the truth of who God is and who we are in light of Him. Like my college professor, the Lord routinely evaluates our spiritual growth. Learning and growing are what the life expedition is all about.

In the time of the exodus, God's people faced a few whirlwind weeks filled with miraculous activity. The Red Sea divided so they could pass through on dry land while Pharaoh's army drowned behind them. The bitter waters of Marah supernaturally became sweet, giving the Hebrews both a source of water and another taste of God's awesome power. The people could see God's ability and experience His love for them as miracles unfolded.

Every time the Israelites encountered God's provision they ran headlong into an opportunity for spiritual growth. Each miraculous moment became a lesson in learning to lean on the Lord. Though they would continue to face difficulty, they would do so in the knowledge that God is both powerful and reliable. He could effectively rescue them from anything.

How has seeing God work in the past impacted your relationship with Him today?

The Lord evaluates spiritual progress because He loves us and desires to see whether we listen to and apply the principles He teaches. This is another reason why God allows the wilderness. He wants to show us that we can't have the benefits and blessings of Canaan without first learning how to walk through the wilderness in dependence and faithfulness. I believe that taking time to review and internalize what God teaches in the barren times is a crucial key to spiritual success.

"For You have tried us, O God; You have refined us as silver is refined."
Psalm 66:10

TEST TIME

One-and-one-half months after their departure from Egypt, God's people faced their third major dilemma. No sooner did they put down their pencils from working their spiritual-growth assignment at Marah than they were called to God's classroom for an exam. In the middle of the wilderness between Elim and Sinai, the people realized they had nothing to eat. They'd learned that God provides, but how would they respond to this test?

Read Exodus 16:1-7. How did the people initially respond to their hunger?

In the margin describe what their response says about how well they'd processed the lessons God taught.

What should the frequency of God's gift have revealed to them about His consistency and love for them?

On your map mark the Wilderness of Sin with a number "3" as the place of God's third miracle for His children.

God allowed the Red Sea circumstance and the bitter disappointment of Marah to strengthen His children's reliance on Him. The lesson? God provides. When the Lord allowed His children to run out of their own supply of food, test time arrived. While they should've known that God's intentions toward them were good, they panicked. Not once had the Father ever left them and not once had He allowed their needs to go unaddressed, yet they seemed to forget His past expressions of love and question His character. Israel miserably failed God's test.

"Examine me, O Lord, and try me; Test my mind and my heart."
Psalm 26:2

List some lessons God has taught you. To the right of each explain how He's tested. I've given an example.

Lesson Taught	Test Given	My Grade
Don't Complain; Trust	Jerry and I experienced financial troubles. Would I complain or relinquish control to God?	C-

For each of these instances, assign yourself a grade (A to F) to signify how well you think you did on the test.

When Jerry and I recently faced a financial crisis, I, much like the children of Israel, immediately fell into a habit of whining about my circumstances. Thankfully, Jerry got tired of it and asked me bluntly whether or not I was going to trust God. His stark comments came as a reality check. Suddenly,

I could see how badly I was failing the test God placed before me. My whining indicated my lack of faith in God's love and His ability to provide.

After seeking the Lord's forgiveness, I thanked Him for giving me the opportunity to put my faith into practice. I asked the Lord to give me a heightened spiritual sensitivity to the divine purpose of life's challenges.

How might the Israelites have responded had they recognized their hunger as a spiritual test?

How might knowing that the Lord tests us alter your response to the next challenge life presents? As you anticipate life's inevitable difficult situations, consider how you can prepare yourself to pass with flying colors.

GOD'S PANTRY

Yahweh allowed the Hebrews to experience inner emptiness that they did not have the ability to fill. He wanted them to experience the abundant supply that only God's pantry can offer. Passing the test meant embracing the hunger and counting on the Lord to fill it. Yet instead of expecting God to meet their needs, the Israelites feared abandonment and starvation. In spite of all God had done, they failed to trust that God proves faithful.

Most assuredly a season of emptiness will accompany your journey to the promised land too. Just as clearly as you recognize your stomach's call for suppertime, you will recognize spiritual hunger. In fact, it's more than just a general hunger; spiritual hunger leaves a soul famished. Understand that God designs and allows spiritual emptiness. Only the Lord can satisfy it.

How do you know when an inner hunger is meant for only God, not someone/something else in your life, to fill?

Prepare to discuss the purpose of spiritual hunger or dissatisfaction with your group.

Yahweh graciously opened the heavenly pantry to satisfy not only their physical needs but also their spiritual hunger for more of Him—a need they didn't even recognize. Scripture says that the Lord "satisfies the longing soul, and the hungry soul he fills with good things" (Ps. 107:9, ESV). You and I must understand that God wants to meet our spiritual hunger too. He wants us to seek to fulfill it by searching the Word, spending time in prayer, and yielding to the Holy Spirit's leading in our lives.

Jesus taught, "Blessed are those who hunger and thirst for righteousness, for they shall be satisfied" (Matt. 5:6). When we seek God's help in filling our spiritual bellies, He happily gives all we need. Consider God's faithfulness in your life. He hears you, loves you, and will not leave you as you travel to His desired destination. Although the journey is not without times of thirst and hunger, God will provide and keep you.

Circle God's words to the people in Exodus 16:12. Underline the part that explains the purpose of God's provision in this instance.

When you find within yourself a gnawing hunger that you can't fill with any relationship, success, or earthly resources, know that God is leading you to an opportunity to better know Him as your Sustainer. When church-as-usual becomes less satisfying and your soul hungers for more than a mere conference or message, know that God calls you to His kitchen.

Don't let the hunger you feel today cause you to complain and forget His past goodness in your life. God allows hunger so that you can know the satisfaction of a full spiritual tank. School is in session, friend. Recognize hunger as God's gift. Remember what you've been learning and apply those lessons when test time comes. Let's prepare to pass with flying colors as we "labor [not] for the food which perishes, but for the food which endures to everlasting life" (John 6:27, NKJV).

"I have heard the grumblings of the sons of Israel; speak to them, saying, 'At twilight you shall eat meat, and in the morning you shall be filled with bread; and you shall know that I am the LORD your God.'"
Exodus 16:12

Day 4
The In-between Times

My boys don't like in-between times. At Disney World they thought they'd die every evening when facing a whole night between one thrilling day at the park and the next. Teaching them patience is one of my most challenging mommy tasks because it is not one of my strengths.

In-between times in our relationships with the Lord are difficult too. If we aren't careful, we become idle between one spiritual high point and the next. These times provide the Enemy the perfect opportunity to convince us that God doesn't love us and has forgotten about us. It allows Satan to dim our memories of God's incredible provision, effectively snuffing out our expectations of what's to come.

God strategically guided the Israelites through the wilderness. With each miracle the Lord showed Himself strong on behalf of His children and wowed them with His great power and love. Between these supernatural displays, however, the people began to twiddle their spiritual thumbs. Discontentment settled as they grumpily waited for God to wow them again.

RECOGNIZING THE IN-BETWEEN

The in-between times should not be despised. They are the necessary connections between one event and the next.

Each of the great miracles Israel experienced occurred after a pause between God's last supernatural display and the next. (Not including, of course, the constant presence of the pillar and cloud.) A time of waiting and patience followed each miracle. The Israelites had to trust in God's love and protection even when the miracles decreased in frequency.

The in-between times should not be despised. They are the necessary connections between one event and the next. The miracle at the Red Sea occurred after God delivered them from Pharoah. The miracle at Marah occurred after God had parted the Red Sea. The miracle in the Wilderness of Sin occurred after they set out from Elim.

"Then they set out from Elim, and all the congregation of the sons of Israel came to the wilderness of Sin, which is between Elim and Sinai, on the fifteenth day of the second month after their departure from the land of Egypt."
Exodus 16:1

On your map, put a question mark between Egypt and the Red Sea, between the Red Sea and Marah, and between Marah and the Wilderness of Sin.

Read Exodus 16:1. Where were the Israelites prior to their stop in the Wilderness of Sin and where would they go upon leaving it?

What miracle did God perform at Elim (15:27)?

Quickly scan Exodus 19:18. What miracle would God work at Sinai?

God evidenced miraculous provision for His children at Elim and would again at Sinai. The passage from one miraculous moment with God to the next, however, required a journey through the in-between.

Why do you think God orchestrates in-between times in our spiritual lives?

As I write this lesson, I am most certainly in an in-between time in my spiritual journey. Yesterday I looked through my journal and smiled as I read of the many miracles God performed in my life between 2004 and 2006. During that season God was on a divine roll. From supernaturally providing desperately needed office furniture to causing my son's birth just as I'd specifically prayed, God wowed me often.

Looking back at that time, I realize that my intimate times with the Lord in those days of miracles were fresh and vibrant. I heard His voice clearly during those spiritual highs and lived in daily awareness of His presence. My love relationship with the Father blazed hot as He repeatedly wowed me with His ability. Lately, however, miracles occur a little less often in the Shirer household. Don't get me wrong. God still does great things for our family. But in this season, He's toned down the wow factor.

I admit this seeming lack of divine intervention makes navigation difficult for a girl who's begun to expect the unexpected and unusual. In this in-between time I'm tempted to ease up on my commitment to prayer and to slack when it comes to personally connecting with God. In all honesty, I struggle against the desire to complain about God's seeming aloofness.

In your life right now, are you:
■ currently seeing God's glory and activity evidenced?
■ at an in-between place in your journey, where nothing much seems to be happening?

In the margin, what part of the in-between times do you find most challenging? How do you respond when miraculous interventions seem few and far between?

How should a believer respond to God when she feels she's experiencing a spiritual lull?
■ take a break from church and focus on Bible study
■ beg for God to wow her spiritually again
■ maintain focus and seek God's direction

RESPONDING TO IN-BETWEEN TIMES

Read Exodus 16:2. How did the Hebrews respond to their in-between time?

The Hebrews allowed fear to overshadow them and began to doubt God's love. Quite literally, they began to grumble. They really thought that the God who loved them enough to deliver them, protect them, and provide for them would leave them stranded in the middle of nowhere. This line of thought parallels our modern tendency. When we can't see signs of God's intervention, we often start to complain.

Compare the episode of grumbling in Exodus 16:2-3 with the previous complaining in Exodus 15:24-25. In the margin list all the ways the two differ.

Notice the intensity of the complaining and whining in the second account. No longer are only "the people" fussing, but the "whole congregation of the sons of Israel" has joined in! At Marah they at least tasted the water before coming to Moses with their problem. Just down the road, however, they started complaining before a problem existed. At Marah they complained only to Moses; now they complained to Moses and Aaron.

Read the following verses. Note the progression of the Hebrews' complaints.

"Our fathers, when they were in Egypt, did not consider your wondrous works; they did not remember the abundance of your steadfast love, but rebelled by the sea, at the Red Sea. … They soon forgot his works; they did not wait for his counsel. … They murmured in their tents, and did not obey the voice of the LORD" (Ps. 106:7,13,25, ESV).

The spirit of complaint often takes this pattern. It begins as frustration and spreads into a raging flame of disgust, whining, and longing for something other than what God provides. Complaining is what kept God's people from passing their spiritual tests. Again and again their gaze proved so tightly focused on what they wished would happen that they despised reality.

Unwilling to recall God's past goodness or anticipate His future activity, they became blind to what God was doing in the now. Israel's faith in God and view of their journey grew distorted, so they ignored truth about God's love and faithfulness. Grumbling blinded them to the fact that the in-between time was part of God's plan. Make no mistake about it—a grumbling spirit will rob you of what God designed the in-between time to teach you. It will keep you from getting the most out of your journey with God. "The right attitude in real difficulty is unconditional acceptance and obedience. God's own must never stand in judgment upon him."[4]

According to Romans 1:21, what happened to the hearts of those who proved unthankful for God's provision?

EMBRACING THE CURE

We must choose to carefully guard our reaction to in-between times. Philippians 2:14 suggests that Christians should "do everything without complaining or arguing" (NIV). That means instead of defaulting to our natural tendency to point out what God is not doing, we should refocus our attention on what He has accomplished and is accomplishing. We must force ourselves to recall the promises He has made, proactively claiming those promises regardless of our feelings. The Lord desires that we spend our days in contemplation of His deliverance and restoration in our lives. When we do, we'll effectively guard our hearts against the tendency to complain.

Paul admonished the Philippian church to "rejoice in the Lord always ... [to] be anxious for nothing, but in everything by prayer and supplication with thanksgiving let your requests be made known to God." He said, "Whatever is true, whatever is honorable, whatever is right, whatever is pure, whatever is lovely, whatever is of good repute, if there is any excellence and if anything is worthy of praise, [let your mind] dwell on these things" (Phil. 4:4,6,8). As you face the frustration of in-between times, purposefully focus on those things Paul advised.

In the previous paragraph, underline the eight principles on which we should think. Circle one and then in the margin write a list of thoughts that could fall under that category regarding something in your life of which you would normally think negatively.

Copy your list onto a note card. The next time you feel the need to complain, take out the card and discipline your mind to focus on the good. Doing so will refocus your attention on God's greatness and ability to provide.

Scripture says that "we must not put Christ to the test, as [Israel] did and were destroyed by serpents, nor grumble, as some of them did and were destroyed by the Destroyer" (1 Cor. 10:9-10, ESV). Grumbling against the Lord's plan for our lives is a serious offense.

Let's determine to trust God for the in-between times. He always proves faithful.

"For even though they knew God, they did not honor Him as God or give thanks, but they became futile in their speculations, and their foolish heart was darkened."
Romans 1:21

As Albert Lindsey so aptly put it, "An unthankful heart eventually becomes dark."[5]

Day 5
A Blessing, Not a Barrier

God's activity during the exodus reveals His deliberate attempts to show Himself mighty. He purposefully "led the people around by the way of the wilderness to the Red Sea," forgoing the easier and more convenient route (Ex. 13:18). He desired not to get the Hebrews in close proximity to Canaan as much as bringing them to close proximity to Himself. The Lord knew that a stint in the wilderness could best accomplish His purpose in the lives of those He loved.

When God chooses wilderness times for us, we should not view them as a barrier to promised-land living. While it's tempting to believe that our excursions in life's barren seasons are a waste of time and a departure from our spiritual objective, they serve a higher purpose. The wilderness is a blessing meant to help us see God more fully and completely, to help us love Him more wholeheartedly, and to show us the importance of committing to Him above all else. The wilderness provides a vital and necessary prerequisite to reaching the spiritual abundance He wants to give. The path through the wilderness is the only route to Canaan for us.

GOD'S GLORY ON DISPLAY
We cannot conclude our discussion of the wilderness' purpose without pausing to explore the most important one.

Read Exodus 14:4. What did the demise of Pharaoh's army bring to the Lord?
- rest
- vengeance
- honor
- a sense of purpose

Explain how the Israelites' time in the wilderness contributed to the fulfillment of this passage.

The English Standard Version presents Exodus 14:4 in this way: "I will harden Pharaoh's heart, and he will pursue them, and I will get glory over Pharaoh and all of his host, and the Egyptians shall know that I am the LORD." The word "glory" here is significant because it gives us a better understanding of what God had in mind for the drama that unfolded at the Red Sea. The original word used is *kabed*, meaning "to be heavy, weighty, or burdensome."[6] It presents the idea of a person whose integrity is given immense weight and credibility and therefore is more fully trusted. By positioning the Hebrews to witness the annihilation of Pharaoh's troops, the Lord gave the Israelites a tremendous visual that helped raise their understanding of just how much honor He is due.

The Lord desires that you experience Him in such a tangible way that it raises His level of credibility with you. God wants for you to give Him, His influence, power, and ability more weight in your life.

How might a more weighty view of God's ability alter your relationship with Him?

Share with your group about a time when your appreciation of God's ability deepened. How did it impact your pursuit of the Lord?

Salvation delivers you out of Egypt, but the wilderness is designed to work Egypt out of you and replace the prominence of its influence in your life with God's. We must encounter and embrace the wilderness in order to align our lives to His plan.

The mind-blowing encounters we'll find in the wilderness will inevitably increase the honor we assign to God. As they do, we'll realize that God wants to have an increasing amount of weight in our decision-making and lifestyle choices. He wants and deserves our allegiance and dependence. As we encounter miracles in the wilderness, our confidence in Him is reinforced. Lovingly, patiently, God works the enslavement of Egypt out of our hearts.

How has God used the wilderness to work Egypt out of you?

How did this impact your relationship with God?

In the chart below record a personal miracle in a difficult time through which God received glory.

Past Wilderness Difficulty	God's Miracle	God's Glory

Think about a current difficulty you face. What kind of miracle might God work in this situation? Explain how God might receive glory through such a miracle.

Wilderness Difficulty	Expected Miracle	God's Glory

Rate the level of difficulty you found in filling in the second chart:

easy   somewhat easy   difficult   I didn't fill it in.

Explain your answer.

By completing the second exercise, you demonstrated a renewed sense of expectation and confidence in God's ability and love for you. Years ago I would've left that activity blank. As I traveled through the wilderness spiritually, I had no spiritual vision or anticipation of God's activity on my behalf. I became so self-consumed, overwhelmed by frustration, eaten alive with impatience, and bogged down by confusion that I often stopped praying, trusting in God, or anticipating His work in my life.

Now that I understand God desires to give Himself more credibility in my eyes by bringing glory to His name, I'm learning to trust that He does indeed work on my behalf regardless of what I might face. In fact, my most difficult moments better allow the Lord to receive honor.

What's the danger in using this dynamic as license to demand miracles?

Understand that we cannot make demands of God and grow disappointed and angry when He doesn't move in the way we expect. While we can pray for specific miracles, we must trust that God will choose to work in a way that both brings Him glory and serves His purposes for our lives. Furthermore, we must recognize that the Lord is not bound to our whims. He is God and we are not. With that in mind, I want to challenge you to make this your prayer: "Lord, this is what I desire. Please do it or something better."

The Christian's prayer in the wilderness: "Lord this is what I desire. Please do it or something better."

If God chooses to do something other than what you have written as your "expected miracle," do you trust that it will be better suited to you and His purposes of bringing credibility to His name in your life and the lives of others?

⬛ yes ⬛ no ⬛ not sure

Take a moment to release control over your difficulties to the Lord, choosing to believe in His overwhelming love for you. Trust Him to decide what is best for you. After you pray, draw a line through your prediction of what kind of miracle God could use to help you through your difficulty. Instead, write across the exercise, "Trust God."

We've got to know that sickness, financial debacles, marital disasters, heartbreaks, and the greatest needs of our lives don't have to derail our relationship with God. In the midst of our pain, God makes a way for us to see and experience His greatness.

1. M.G. Easton. *Easton's Bible Dictionary* (Oak Harbor, WA: Logos Research Systems, 1996).
2. John D. Currid. *Ancient Egypt and the Old Testament* (Grand Rapids, MI: Baker Books, 1997), 145, quoted in Dorian Coover Cox, "How Will It Be Known?" *The Art of Characterization in the Book of Exodus* (Dallas, 2001), 199.
3. Philip Graham Ryken. *Exodus: Saved for God's Glory* (Wheaton, IL: Crossway Books, 2005), 416.
4. R. Laird Harris. ed., *Theological Wordbook of the Old Testament* (Chicago: Moody Press, 1980), 1:1101.
5. Albert Lindsey. *Wilderness Experiences* (Metropolitan Printing Co, 1973), 51–52.
6. Robert L. Thomas. *New American Standard Hebrew-Aramaic and Greek Dictionaries,* Updated Edition (Anaheim, CA: Foundation Publications, 1998), H. 3513.

Session 4
Viewer Guide

Our responsibility is not to figure out or fix the wilderness. Our responsibility is to __*yield*__ to the wilderness.

Exodus 13:17-18
"Now when Pharaoh had let the people go, God did not lead them by the way of the land of the Philistines, even though it was near; for God said, 'The people might change their minds when they see war, and return to Egypt.' Hence God led the people around by the way of the wilderness to the Red Sea; and the sons of Israel went up in martial array from the land of Egypt."

"Therefore"   *need to look back at what came before the "therefore"*

The "therefore" is the connecting link between the hugeness of our sin and the far greater enormity of His love for us in spite of that sin.

most Romantic book in Bible

The wilderness reveals to us:

1. The __*passion*__ of God

Hosea 2:14
"Therefore, behold, I will allure her,
Bring her into the wilderness
And speak kindly to her."

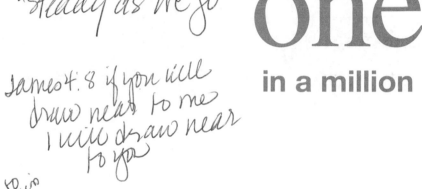

"Steady as we go"

one
in a million

James 4:8 if you will draw near to me I will draw near to you

as Him

Allure: to entice by charm; to attract

speak kindly to us

comfort us with love + presence

Romans 8:18

"For I consider that the sufferings of this present time are not worthy to be compared with the glory that is to be revealed to us."

Intimacy with us is God's _goal_.

make a decision to cling when chaos is all around

2. The _power_ of God

3. The _purpose_ of God

The same _God Yahweh_ who was willing to pay a price for His beloved people in the Old Testament is the same God who loved us so much He was _willing to pay great ___ _with price___ in the New Testament.

He was willing to send His _only_ begotten Son to die on the cross of Calvary.

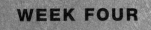

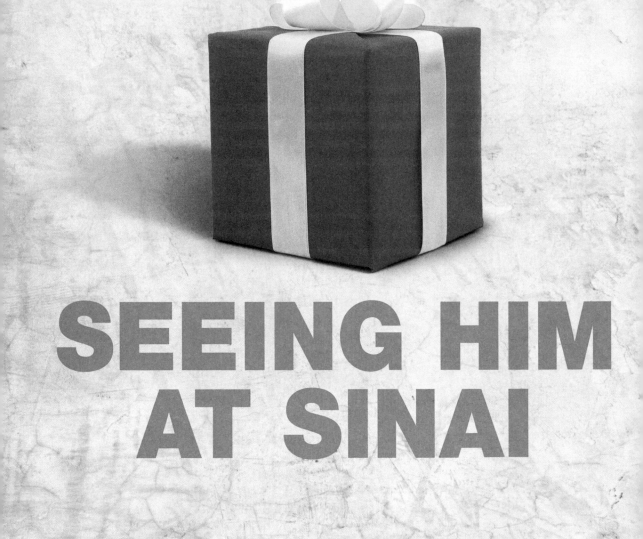

SEEING HIM AT SINAI

During my childhood, Mom and Dad would sometimes leave for about a week to share the gospel in a foreign country. They developed the habit of bringing home a little trinket for each of us. While my siblings and I would miss them, we consoled ourselves with the knowledge that they would soon return bearing gifts.

When we heard their car pulling into the driveway, we'd rush outside and nearly flatten them with enthusiastic welcome. I remember my father's face lighting with glee at the sight of us, only to dim into a somber frown when we'd greedily beg for our presents. The two weary travelers hadn't gathered their belongings from the trunk when a chorus of, "What'd you get me? What does it do? What does it say? Can I have it now?" arose. I'll never forget how, when asked to give them a moment to collect themselves, we slumped our shoulders and, I'm ashamed to admit, endlessly whined for our presents.

Not until years later did Mom mention how much our greed hurt Daddy. He'd spend hours looking forward to getting back to Dallas to see us only to find that all his kids really wanted were the toys he bought.

I now know how it feels to have one's gifts preferred over her presence. My boys no longer wait for my return. They look for the shopping bags stuffed in my luggage.

Day 1
Igniting Intimacy

The Lord longs for intimacy with His people and wants us to hunger for it too. We should desire Him above all else. God will do whatever it takes to keep our minds purposed on this goal—even if that means delaying the satisfaction of Canaan. Whether we find ourselves in the midst of a desert or enjoying an oasis of plenty, God's purpose is to develop passionate hearts that beat for Him.

"[He] is a God who is jealous about his relationship with you."
Exodus 34:14, NLT

Rate the heat level of your passion for God right now.

cold	tepid	warm	boiling over

How does your life testify to this passion or the lack of it?

Would those who know you best agree with your answer? Why or why not?

Exodus 19 introduces one of the most pivotal settings in Israel's history. Three months after leaving Egypt, God led the Israelites into the wilderness of Sinai, in the midst of which stood a rocky precipice. That imposing mountain served as the focal point of their attention for approximately one year.

Sinai was no ordinary mountain. It was considered so holy that many referred to it not by its geographical name but by another title.

"You yourselves have seen what I did to the Egyptians, and how I bore you on eagles' wings, and brought you to Myself. Now then, if you will indeed obey My voice and keep My covenant, then you shall be My own posses- sion among all the peoples, for all the earth is Mine; and you shall be to Me a king- dom of priests and a holy nation. These are the words that you shall speak to the sons of Israel."
Exodus 19:4-6

According to Exodus 3:1 and 24:13, what holy name was given to this site? *M.O.G.*

Turn to your map. Write "M.O.G." for "Mountain of God" over the Sinai Peninsula.

Mount Sinai became the place where God would bring them to Himself and set out to inflame His people with zeal for Him. The primary reason why God allowed the wilderness was to bring them to this place, where the process of intimacy would begin. This is not merely the high point of the exodus of the ancient Hebrews; it is the high point of ours. He saved you from slavery and has led you on this journey you've traveled so that you can meet Him in a unique way at your own "Mountain of God." This is His primary purpose. At Sinai, the children of Israel would ...

hear His voice;

see an outward manifestation of His glory;

be called into full commitment to Him;

be established as His chosen people;

be invited into covenant relationship.

Read Exodus 19:4-6, a passage often described as the heart of the Old Testament. Fill in the blanks from verse 4.

You yourselves have seen *what I did to Egypt*,
and how I *bore you on eagles wings*,
and *brought you to myself*.

God's entire relationship with Israel can be summed up in three distinct proclamations from this verse:
1. a delivering from *[handwritten]*
2. a lifting up *[handwritten]*
3. a bringing unto *[handwritten]*

Yahweh's actions toward His people covered their past, present, and future. The Lord had delivered them from Egypt. He was lifting them up among all other peoples as a nation chosen for His purposes. And He would bring them to Himself, making them a holy nation and a kingdom of priests.

ON EAGLES' WINGS

In week 1 we studied God delivering His people from Egypt. He reminded the people of this as He invited them into relationship with Himself and then turned their attention to their present circumstances. He used beautiful imagery, claiming that He'd sustained Israel "on eagles' wings."

The terminology brings to mind a picture of young birds in need of mom's protection. In Deuteronomy 32 Moses sang a love song about God's care for His people during their time in the desert. In the margin notice the nurturing terminology the Lord assigned to His actions.

Eaglets are helpless, needy animals that depend on the fierce concern and protection of their mothers. They stay in the nest for a long period of time, and the mother ferociously defends them while they mature.

According to one source, when it is time for the young birds to learn to fly, "the eagle stirs up the nest, but does not abandon her young. If they experience difficulties, the mother bird swoops down below them and lifts them on its wings back to safety."[1] Mother eagles love and cherish their young, determine when to stir the nest to incite the desire for flight, and prioritize protecting them as they develop strength.

"The LORD's portion is His people, Jacob, His own inheritance. He found him in a desolate land, in a barren, howling wilderness; He surrounded him, cared for him, and guarded him as the [apple] of His eye. He watches over His nest like an eagle and hovers over His young; He spread His wings, catches him, and lifts him up on His pinions."

Deuteronomy 32:9-11, HCSB

How does our relationship with God compare with the eagle and her young? Consider the following areas, making comparisons for each one.

needy and dependent eaglets

eagle stirring the nest

eagle protecting her young while they learn to fly

COME TO ME

When God spoke to the people about their future, which was to start right there at the mountain of God, He explained the most important part of their salvation experience. The exodus was for this moment—when God's people would be brought unto Himself and begin intimate fellowship and covenant with Him. This was His goal above getting them to Canaan.

Which best describes what God desired to accomplish between Himself and the Israelites?

intimacy

- mutual respect
- a parent-child relationship
- fellowship
- other: _____

What priorities do you think have taken precedence over intimacy with God in Christianity today?

The Lord wants to bring you to a Sinai so your encounter with Him will forever mark and radically change you. Your wilderness experience is to bring you to remember what Christ did for you, acknowledge what He currently is doing, and recommit to personal intimacy with Him.

For the past three years I've attended a home Bible study led by a gifted teacher. During a series of messages on intimacy with God, he quoted American philosopher, Sam Pascoe: "Christianity began in Palestine as a fellowship (a relationship) and then moved to Greece and became a philosophy (way to think). Afterward, it moved onto Rome and became an institution (a place you go) and then to Europe where it became a culture (a way of life). Finally it settled in America where it has become an enterprise (a business)."

How do you see the truth of this statement reflected in modern American Christianity? in your own life?

mega churches - not pursuing saving souls

What can you do to keep your faith based in relationship?

Natalie Grant / Healer Phil 4:13

If you find that this passion is waning in your heart, then share your honest feelings with the Father. Thankfully, God graciously works to stir in us a fresh passion for Him. He took the initiative with Israel and will do the same with you. Just ask Him to draw you to a mountain-of-God moment. There, by His Holy Spirit, He will stir your heart to desire Him above His gifts and to seek His friendship over His blessings.

Day 2
The Sinai Experience

Jordan was a bright, rambunctious boy of nine when he had his first seizure. A trip to the doctor revealed a seemingly inoperable brain tumor. Jordan's parents gave him the prescribed medication to help stop the seizures, but their hope waned quickly. Every time Jordan had a spell, his memory dimmed. He lost words and began to make up his own sign language to compensate.

In emotional agony over their son's illness, Jordan's parents asked God how He could allow this to happen to their little boy. How could He possibly receive glory through their awful situation?

Looking back on those tumultuous months, Jordan's mother notes: "That experience required me to lay down my independence and depend instead on God. I learned that while I may have desired to give everything to God, I held on to the things I thought I could take care of—my little boy included. As Jordan's tumor grew, though, I had no choice but to let go and let God. As a result, I learned that God has a master plan far better than anything I could imagine."

To this family's joy, God provided a surgeon determined to remove Jordan's tumor. Jordan is now a happy, healthy young man with no trace of the illness he suffered.

During one of the most tragic seasons of her life, Jordan's mom experienced Sinai—the place where she saw God in a new way and became more deeply committed to Him. Though each of our circumstances may be different, this is the turn that all of our journeys must take: toward a mountain of experience with God that draws us into divine fellowship like never before.

Describe a time when you saw God during a trying season of your life. How did your view of Him change?

While in college, I was in a relationship that I felt certain would end in marriage. I became devastated when the relationship ended. Over the next weeks, emotional upheaval threatened my health. At my lowest point, I drove down Highway 75 in Dallas, crying so hard that I could barely see. When I pulled over and buried my face in my hands, my heart ached so badly that I begged God to restore the relationship I'd lost.

*"In the third
month after the
sons of Israel
had gone out
of the land of
Egypt, on that
very day they
came into the
wilderness of
Sinai. When
they set out
from Rephidim,
they came to
the wilderness
of Sinai and
camped in the
wilderness; and
there Israel
camped in front
of the mountain."*

Exodus 19:1-2

To my surprise, I heard the Holy Spirit's gentle reply to my request: "Priscilla, he doesn't want you, and you still want a relationship with him. I do want you, Priscilla. Why don't you want a relationship with Me?"

Through my tears, I saw the mountain of God. That moment was my Sinai, the place where God called me into a more intimate relationship with Him. Sadly, it took personal devastation to make my heart sensitive enough to realize it was time to stop thinking about me and to start thinking about God.

List two people you know whose difficult circumstances led them into more intimate relationships with the Lord. Describe the circumstances surrounding their Sinais.

1.

2.

In Exodus 19:1-2, why do you think God allowed three months of hardship prior to their stop at Sinai?

prepare them for intervention

Sometimes we have to wade through a time of difficulty under God's protective guidance before our hearts soften to His invitation to walk with Him. In Hosea 5:15 the Lord said of the wayward Israelites, "I'll go back to where I came from until they come to their senses. When they finally hit rock bottom, maybe they'll come looking for me" (MSG). Sometimes God allows hardship to graciously show us we desperately need Him.

Recall a time when you sought God as a result of a difficult time in your life. In the margin note what you learned from this experience about God and about yourself. Prepare to share this with your group.

Turn to your map and find Mount Sinai. Note its position in relation to Israel's desired destination of Canaan.

Mount Sinai was south. Canaan was far to the north. At the mountain of God, the Israelites were far from the place they desired. No milk or honey was in sight. But while the Hebrews longed for a land of external blessing and abundance, God called them to stop at Sinai. There they would discover internal blessings and an abundance that they didn't realize they needed. At Sinai they obtained intimacy and fellowship with the Lover of their souls, a gift far more precious and lasting than Canaan's milk and honey.

I believe every wilderness journey leads to a Sinai experience. The place that seems distant from your desired destination provides fertile soil for God to reveal Himself to you. Do you think the Hebrews paid more attention to the Lord's words at Sinai than they would have if He had waited to present His offer of relationship once they entered Canaan?

My sister, a walk through the "far-removed-from-our-desires" is not a requirement for intimacy, but it does seem to prepare us for a new level in our relationship with God. Often when we are at our lowest place physically, financially, relationally, or in another crucial area of our lives, God ignites our hearts for Him in a brand new way.

RETURNING TO SINAI

I find it interesting that Moses was no stranger to Sinai. He'd visited Horeb before. When Moses was 40, he ran for his life after killing an Egyptian. Moses fled into the desert where he acquired a new wife and a new identity before ending up at Sinai.

> **Read Exodus 3:1-5,10 and answer the following: What was Moses doing in the wilderness (v. 1)?**
>
> *tending Jethro's sheep*
>
> **What supernatural occurrence took place there (vv. 2-4)?**
>
> *burning bush*
>
> **What adjective did the Lord assign to the land (v. 5)?**
> ▨ rocky   ▨ rich   ☒ holy
>
> **What mission did God assign to Moses (v. 10)?**
>
> *go to pharaoh let my people go*

In Exodus 3:12 God gave Moses the promise of a sign. Just as the Lord had promised, Moses found himself standing on Sinai's holy soil. This time, however, Moses knew how to respond at the mountain of God. He recalled that during one of the most unsure, uncomfortable seasons of his life, God supernaturally intervened and called him into a relationship. That moment altered the mission of Moses' entire existence. No longer was he a prince of Egypt. Now he was a friend of God.

Moses knew from past experience that encountering the mountain of God could change a life. Now, he led the nation to pitch their tents and settle in to see what God would do in this place.

"This shall be the sign to you that it is I who have sent you: when you have brought the people out of Egypt, you shall worship God at this mountain."
Exodus 3:12

Look at Exodus 19:2. What did Israel do in front of the mountain of God?

When I'm in the wilderness of uncertainty, the last thing I want to do is pitch my tent and camp. I don't want to settle in and get comfortable with that part of the journey. My inclination is to escape the shadow of God's guidance, run ahead of Him, and get out of there as soon as possible. But notice that when the Israelites came to the mountain of God, they "camped" out to experience all that God would have for them there (Ex. 19:2).

Imagine two million refugees unpacking their knapsacks, pitching their tents, and corralling their livestock for an extended stay in a place they really didn't want to be. In spite of their eagerness to reach Canaan and in spite of all of questions and frustrations, Israel obediently waited and rested before the mountain of God. I think we can learn from their example.

Complete the following statement. In a difficult season allowed by God to reveal Himself, I'm usually inclined to:
- **acknowledge Him for a moment and then try to move forward expediently**
- **"camp out" to see what He wants to do in me**
- **grow impatient and miss what God is doing**

On page 38 you wrote down the questions you've been asking God about this season of your life. Look back at those questions and consider the following:

Are you frustrated by them and the delay in receiving a response from God regarding them? ▨ **yes** ▨ **no**

Have you ever considered that this time of questioning is part of the journey God has you on and that He is not upset with you for asking them? ▨ **yes** ▨ **no**

What would it look like for you to camp at this place in your journey? How would that change your actions and emotions in the next few days?

While I am certainly still on my journey with God and have much to learn and experience with Him, I want to offer you the encouragement that Moses undoubtedly offered as Israel waited at the mountain's base. Friend, camp at this mountain with a glad heart. Despite the difficulty of the journey and with all of your questions in tow, fully engage in this season of God's chosen journey for you. Don't leave your bags packed in hopes God will quickly move you to Canaan. Don't miss out on what He wants to do "this very day" (Ex. 19:1). Settle in and turn your eyes to the mountain. The Lord wants to reveal Himself to you in a way that will change your life forever.

Earlier you listed two people who encountered God in unique ways during devastating seasons. Contact one of them this week, asking him or her to encourage you as you camp out at Sinai. Record highlights from your conversation in the margin.

Day 3
Covenant Commitments

Four-month-old Jackson fell asleep on his father's lap on a flight. Then our little one began to reek with the unmistakable odor of a diaper filled. Jerry's face, so peaceful only moments before, contorted in a grimace as he held his beloved boy at arm's length.

I grabbed a diaper and disappeared into the airplane bathroom to do damage control. To my dismay, I discovered a "blow out." The stinky disaster required a head-to-toe change leaving that little room smelling beyond foul. When I finally emerged from the tiny restroom, feeling badly for the person who would next enter, I returned Jackson to his father's arms. Jerry cradled his sweet-smelling infant closely for the rest of the flight. The yucky stench no longer came between them.

To us God says, "Draw near to [Me], and [I] will draw near to you" (Jas. 4:8). He wants to pull us near but closeness between us and the Father is impossible without the divine intervention called grace. Unholy humans cannot fellowship with a holy God as long as the filthy stench of sin hovers around our lives. When our souls stink with the putrid odor of rebellion, the Father is forced to hold us at arm's length.

Yahweh wanted to do for His people something He had never done for any other. He wanted to make Israel His holy nation, a nation set apart for His services and purposes. He also wanted them as His treasured possession, meaning that every person would be highly valued and cherished. The Lord wanted the Israelites to serve as His kingdom of priests, meaning every

"For you are a people, holy to the Lord your God and the Lord has chosen you to be a people for His treasured possession, out of all the people who are on the face of the earth."
Deuteronomy 14:2

89

individual would have full access to God and would serve as His ambassadors to the world. He desires the same for New Testament believers.

> Read 1 Peter 2:9. In the margin list three truths that connect New Testament believers with ancient Israel.
>
> *called to be holy.*
>
> How does Isaiah 59:2 shed light on how sin impacts God's plans for His children?

When we accept Christ, God adopts us into His family. If we continue to sin against Him, He still loves us but He restricts fellowship with us. He creates Sinai experiences to refocus our attention on God. They cause us to desire Him more than the sin and selfishness that pollute our relationship.

When the people arrived at Sinai, God revealed the benefits acquired by righteous living. Exodus 19:5-6 presents a call to *holiness*—to *set apart-ness*. Holiness connotes the idea of living in dedication and devotion to God's service. While the thought of trading in our stinky sin tendencies to live in holiness may seem impossible, Scripture encourages us that the goal is attain-able. The Lord will help us achieve holiness by guiding us with the power of the Holy Spirit.

> Which of the following statements best describes your feelings toward the call to holiness?
> - an overwhelming calling
> - a frustrating mission
> - an unattainable goal
> - a joy to pursue
> - a burdensome aspiration

> In the margin describe what Ezekiel 36:25-27 reveals about the Spirit's role in living a life of holiness.
>
> *new heart, new spirit help us*

GOD'S COVENANT

God chose Israel, freed them from bondage, and sustained them through their wilderness journey. God did this as a result of His unconditional cove-nant with their forefather, Abraham. The term covenant is *berith* in Hebrew and "is a promise or an agreement between God and man."[2]

There are two types of covenants: conditional or unconditional. The type of *berith* between God and Abraham in Genesis 12 and 13 is unconditional. In the unconditional covenant, the terms of the agreement are not dependent on the other party's commitment to follow through. Instead, it is completely dependent on God's unwavering steadfastness.

By the time they reached Sinai, the children of Israel could no longer ride the coattails of their forefathers' faith. They needed to make their own personal commitment to the Lord. In this situation, the Lord extended a conditional covenant (Ex. 19:5-6). Two key words show a conditional covenant: if and then. This type of covenant implies a responsibility on man's side of the fence before the Lord is expected to follow through on His end of the deal.

All biblical covenants are initiated by God, not by humans. They come as an act of God's grace and kindness extended toward people who do not even deserve a divine glance. Understand, then, that the decision whether or not to offer the agreement without conditions is up to God. In Israel's case, "obedience to the commands of the law was to be rewarded by God's constant care of Israel, temporal prosperity, victory over enemies, and the pouring out of His Spirit (Ex. 23:20-33)."[3] God expected their loyalty in return.

Eight important covenants appear in the Bible:
- the covenant with repentant sinners—*Hebrews 13:20 (unconditional)*
- the covenant with Adam—*Genesis 1–3 (conditional)*
- the covenant with Noah—*Genesis 8:21-22 (unconditional)*
- the covenant with Abraham—*Genesis 12:2-3,7 (unconditional)*
- the covenant with Moses and Israel—*Deuteronomy 28 (conditional)*
- the covenant with David—*2 Samuel 23:5 (unconditional)*
- the covenant with the church—*Matthew 26:28 (unconditional)*
- the new covenant—*Hebrews 8:7-12 (unconditional)*

Consider the unconditional nature of the covenant God extends to the church. As a believer and member of His church, you've been given an unconditional promise of a permanent standing of righteousness before God. We have fellowship, connection, and covenant with Him only because He first desired these things with us. Knowing this should be the catalyst that thrusts us forward into the pursuit of holiness in our everyday living.

How would our lives be different if our covenant with God was conditional?

In the margin describe how knowing your covenant is unconditional affects your desire to pursue holiness.

CHRIST HAS COME!
When God told the Hebrews to obey His laws, He referred to the Mosaic law. These were 10 commandments, which were a temporary covenant purposed to protect the people from the wrath of a holy God only until a greater, more substantial pledge was given. Galatians 3 teaches us:

"Before the way of faith in Christ was available to us, we were placed under guard by the law. We were kept in protective custody, so to speak, until the way of faith was revealed. Let me put it another way. The law was our guardian until Christ came; it protected us until we could be made right with God through faith. ... Now that you belong to Christ, you are the true children of Abraham. You are his heirs, and God's promise to Abraham belongs to you." **Galatians 3:23-24,29,** NLT

Hear that again: Christ has come! We are no longer under the law, which served as a mirror that showed disobedience but couldn't help fix it. Grace extended to us through Christ's blood and the indwelling Holy Spirit empowers us to walk in holiness as we yield to His control.

The children of Israel had to obey God's voice to receive the benefits Yahweh offered in the Mosaic covenant at Sinai. I believe that the sheer joy of knowing all that God had done for them in spite of their shortcomings and disobedience should have glued them to His side.

As believers and members of His church, we have received an unconditional promise of a permanent standing of righteousness before God. We have fellowship with Him, connection with Him, and covenant with Him only because He first desired those things with us. The facts should stir us to action. We should exclaim as the children of Israel did, "All that the LORD has spoken we will do" (Ex. 19:8) as our hearts overflow with love for the One who first loved us.

"Investigate my life, O God, find out everything about me; Cross-examine and test me, get a clear picture of what I'm about; See for yourself whether I've done anything wrong—then guide me on the road to eternal life."
Psalm 139:23-24, THE MESSAGE

How does all the Lord has done for you affect your attitude toward His call to holiness?

As you conclude today's lesson, pray the words of the psalmist in Psalm 139 and answer the following: Are you knowingly living in rebellion against God in any area of your life? ▓ yes ▓ no

If you answered yes, are you willing to choose holiness in all areas? ▓ yes ▓ no

What practical steps can you take to turn away from anything that keeps you from pursuing holiness? Plan to discuss these with your group.

Day 4
Not Seeing Is Believing

In Liz Curtis Higgs' book, *Embrace Grace,* she makes this startling comment. "So much for the old [proverb] 'Seeing is believing.' God says, 'Not seeing is believing.' "[4]

Not Seeing is Believing? I always want a little proof before believing something. Yet Hebrews 11:1 supports the observation: "Faith is being sure of what we hope for and certain of what we do not see" (NIV). Believing God means having faith in God's Word even when you lack visual evidence. Are you more inclined to see and then believe or believe and then trust God to show you?

The words of this proverb rang in my heart while sitting in the audience at a Christian conference. I felt prompted to give a financial gift to a woman who had spent 25 years in faithful ministry. At the time, Jerry and I were in financial need ourselves and giving didn't make sense. I didn't even know this woman well and yet the internal nagging persisted. I consulted with Jerry and we decided to just act on what we thought God was saying and have faith that He would provide for us. We gave her all the cash we had on us.

When we got home, at our front door we found an envelope from an old friend we'd lent money to years before—so long ago that we had completely forgotten. Inside the envelope was the exact amount we had just given.

Tears welled up in my eyes. God had graciously confirmed our decision to obey Him before we could see proof that He would provide.

I'm just learning to trust God with a radical faith. Instances like this one encourage me to be more consistent. I've long admired believing women who don't have to see God's hand to believe He is who He declares Himself to be and can do what He says. I suspect, though, that I'm not the only person who struggles with trusting God when I can't catch a glimpse of what He's up to.

Exodus 19 reveals God's choice to speak in a way that all could hear Him. What other ways did God give His people tangible evidence of His presence (Ex. 19:18-19)?

God knew that the children of Israel struggled with this as well, so at Sinai God once again performed the miraculous to boost their trust in Him and allegiance to Him. Today's passage is so important because it shows us that God wanted to gain the trust of the people and that He would do it in two ways: by letting the people see Him and by letting the people hear Him.

"All the people answered together and said, 'All that the LORD has spoken we will do!' And Moses brought back the words of the people to the LORD. The LORD said to Moses, 'Behold, I will come to you in a thick cloud, so that the people may hear when I speak with you and may also believe in you forever.' Then Moses told the words of the people to the LORD."
Exodus 19:8-9

The Lord prepared to reveal the Ten Commandments to Moses but first He made an unusual decision. To ensure that the people would accept the validity of the laws, God made Himself seen and heard by the entire multitude. God desires for His children to hear His voice and see His activity. Today we will consider the concept of hearing God; tomorrow we will discuss seeing God.

ON HEARING GOD

Which of these statements describe your understanding of the idea that God's speaks. Check all that apply.
- **I believe God audibly spoke only in biblical times.**
- **I believe God speaks to modern believers through circumstances.**
- **I believe God speaks only to full-time ministers.**
- **I believe God speaks through His living Word.**
- **I believe God is always speaking; we just don't listen.**
- **I believe God speaks to our hearts through His Spirit.**

Plan to discuss your responses with your group this week.

"What other nation is so great as to have their gods near them the way the Lord our God is near us whenever we pray to him? Remember the day you stood before the Lord your God at Horeb, when he said to me, 'Assemble the people before me to hear my words so that they may learn to revere me as long as they live in the land and may teach them to their children.'"
Deuteronomy 4:7,10, NIV

Exodus 19 suggests that God spoke audibly in this situation. Some scholars say that the Lord spoke to Moses through some kind of inward, private inspiration. But in that case, how would the people have heard God?

While I've never heard God's audible voice, I don't think the point of the Israelites' encounter at Sinai is *how* they heard God but *that* they heard Him. God wanted to be certain His people heard Him and chose the most appropriate means to make sure that happened. The illustration we find in Exodus 19 should shed light on the lengths to which He'll go to make His voice clear.

Why do you think God chose to let the Israelites hear Him while in the wilderness so far away from the promised land?

I've found that many times in my life, God's voice became louder during the wilderness of my uncertainty. I'm a better listener when He has my full attention because of difficult circumstances. I believe God spoke to the Israelites during this point in their journey because He knew that their hearts were tender and their spiritual ears were sensitive. His amplified words to Moses gave them an awareness of His presence and His desire for a personal relationship. As a result, they emerged from that season of their lives with a greater reverence for God, a more comprehensive and confident ability to discern God's leading for themselves and a better ability to believe Him even before seeing proof that obedience would pay off.

The Israelites did not have access to God's written Word. In fact, most of it was not written yet. With this in mind, what advantages or disadvantages did the ancient Hebrews have over modern believers in regards to discerning the voice of God? Explain in the margin.

Since we serve a God who desires for us to hear Him throughout our lives, He will often allow wilderness journeys to position us so our spiritual ears are more receptive to His message. God wants you to know His voice with confidence. During the wilderness time in your life, don't start neglecting God's voice. This is prime opportunity for you to lean in, open your ears, and listen. With the Scriptures as your guide, you have every opportunity to clearly discern His leading. Through the power of the Holy Spirit, God will lead and guide you. As you hear Him for yourself, your faith will increase so that you can believe even when—especially—when you cannot see.

HEARING GOD FOR OURSELVES

The children of Israel had access to what God had to say prior to their experience at Sinai. For years God's words had reached their ears through Moses. The problem was not that they couldn't receive God's word; the problem was that they didn't want to receive it personally.

Does the idea of hearing God for yourself:
☐ scare you ☐ excite you ☐ interest you
☐ overwhelm you ☐ seem impossible to you

Read Exodus 20:18-19. How did the people respond to their opportunity to hear from God personally?

When God pitched His tent at the top of the mountain, His people pitched theirs at the bottom. There they grew accustomed to having Moses meet with God in their stead. Satisfied with the safe distance between them and the cloud of God's glory, they settled for less than a face-to-face encounter with their mighty Deliverer. I think Christians still tend to "stand at a distance" and wait to hear from God through pastors and leaders instead of seeking a more personal encounter with God. Why do you suppose we settle for so little?

What does John 16:13 reveal about why believers can hear God for themselves?

Do you tend to depend on someone else to reveal God's word to you? ▪ yes ▪ no If so, who is it and why have you become dependent on them?

God wanted to jumpstart intimate communication with each individual in the Hebrew camp and He used the wilderness to create the right setting to do it. When we find ourselves in the wilderness we can be sure He wants to jumpstart it with us as well! This is what your Sinai experience is all about.

The wonderful message taught by your pastor, stirring thoughts shared by your Sunday School teacher, or encouraging words given by a godly friend may be edifying, but we must not allow them to replace our desire to hear from God for ourselves. In addition to what God may teach us through those whom He places in our lives, you and I need a personal connection with the Lord.

Jesus described His relationship with us in John 10:27: "My sheep hear My voice, and I know them, and they follow Me." The ancient Middle Eastern shepherd's relationship with his sheep was complex and intimate. Without a shepherd's loving guidance, the sheep would stumble upon disaster and perish. When a shepherd found that a particular lamb refused to obey, he would break the rebellious lamb's leg so that it would need to be carried. Slung across the shoulders of his shepherd, the lamb became accustomed to the voice of the shepherd in a new way. When healed, the lamb followed the shepherd without question. Why? Because during a season of pain he'd become acquainted with the voice of the one who loved him.

"[God] tends His flock like a shepherd: He gathers the lambs in his arms and carries them close to his heart."
Isaiah 40:11, NIV

Have you become complacent in hearing and discerning the voice of God in your life? In what way? In the margin write one step you might take to remedy the situation.

OBEDIENCE FIRST

Many want to hear God and see Him in supernatural ways in their lives, but few are willing to pay the price necessary to have ongoing communication with Him. That price is laid out for us in the Israelites' actions in Exodus 19:8.

Read Exodus 19:8. Circle the people's commitment.

Obedience to God was a requirement if the people were to receive the benefits of their covenant relationship with Him. Only after their commitment did God offer to let them hear Him clearly. For the first time, while in the wilderness, the Hebrew children got to experience the voice of God for themselves.

Veiled by a thick black cloud, God revealed His voice in a way His children would never forget. Likewise, while we are in the wilderness God can and will speak to us. We must choose to commit to obedience if we want to walk in the fullness of an intimate relationship with Him. Without our obedience, we will find that our connection with Him seems distant and out of sorts. God wants us to hear Him. The question is, will we listen and will we obediently do all He tells us in order to hear Him more clearly?

My friend, don't wait until things change to start opening your spiritual ears. He wants to speak to you right now. Take the time to commit to obedience. Whatever God prompts you to do, be willing to do it. The more fully you set your heart to follow Him the clearer His voice will become.

> *"All the people answered together and said, 'All that the Lord has spoken we will do!' And Moses brought back the words of the people to the Lord."*
> **Exodus 19:8**

> *"Jesus said to him, 'Because you have seen Me, have you believed? Blessed are they who did not see, and yet believed.'"*
> **John 20:29**

Day 5
Regarding Him with Honor

ALL HAIL THE KING

Grant, a man employed at Hillsong Church where I was speaking at a women's conference, picked us up from London's Heathrow airport. Delighting in his accent and thrilled to be in England, I couldn't help but ask him about her majesty, Queen Elizabeth. My knowledge of her was limited to what the American media dispensed on the news. I wanted to know how she really lives. How do her subjects view her?

Grant explained that while a growing number of younger constituents had less reverence for the queen than in times gone by, overarching feelings of respect for her and the royal family continue throughout Britain. Homage and honor are paid to her by anyone in her presence. Although recent attempts have tried to "normalize" the Queen in England's eyes, no personal or casual relationship exists between the common Londoner and Her Majesty. Distinct honor is given England's royalty.

one

Transcendence:
God is distinct,
above and
separate from
all earthly and
heavenly creation.
Immanence: God
is everywhere
present with His
creation, sustain-
ing it by its pres-
ence and power.[5]

At times during the church's history our view of God has been much like England's view of her queen. Cathedrals built to honor the holiness and majesty of God only emphasized the distance and separateness from us mortals. This emphasis on God's transcendence, or separateness from creation, often kept Christians from personalizing their relationship with Him. It fostered disbelief that they could have ongoing, intimate fellowship with Him.

At other seasons of the church, God's immanence was underscored and His transcendence minimized. Immanence emphasizes the relational and personal involvement of God with His people, but it tended to tone down language regarding the honor due Him. The truth is that God is transcendent and immanent, the perfect balance of both.

In the margin, and in your own words, describe the difference between transcendence and immanence.

Do you tend to see God as more
▨ transcendent   or   ▨ immanent

Which attribute is most highlighted by your church?

your friends?

your family?

Developing a healthy balance between these two parts of God's nature can feel difficult. Casual Christianity has subtly crept into the church, showing itself in an often careless commitment to church attendance and participation in ministry activity. It is evidenced in a lazy approach to spending time with God and a lax attitude towards obedience to Him.

The purpose of
seeing God in
His transcen-
dence is to foster
reverence for His
immanence.

As we neglect the Lord's transcendence, we allow Almighty God to become so personal that we treat Him more like a casual friend than our holy God. We must remember that He is intolerant of rebellion and is character-ized by His wrath and justice just as much as by His mercy and grace. Do not, however, allow yourself to undervalue God's interest in our lives. Though He is incredibly holy and all-powerful, He chooses to seek a relationship with us.

What practical steps can you take to honor God's transcendence and relate to His immanence in your life?

THE BALANCING ACT

We can see the importance of finding balance between friendship with God while still living in awe of Him by looking at God's activity in the sight of all the Hebrews gathered around His holy mountain. He invited them into intimacy and extended an opportunity to hear His voice personally, but He insisted on a reminder of His holiness before giving them the laws that would govern their lives.

> **Read Exodus 19:10-13 and briefly summarize the main idea of each verse.**
> **Verse 10:**
>
> **Verse 11:**
>
> **Verse 12:**
>
> **Verse 13:**

Before God would descend to the mountain, He demanded that His people consecrate themselves. The action was so important that it took three days to complete. The outward action of washing clothes symbolized what must take place in the Israelites' hearts (Lev. 15:5; Gen. 35:2). They could not encounter God with a nonchalant attitude about their sin.

The clear physical boundaries around the mountain also served to remind the people that God cannot be treated with casual indifference. Though He revealed His immanence, God would not sacrifice His transcendence. Both had to be held in high esteem. Believing that God would come, the people acted according to the word of Moses.

> **Look up two of the following passages. Record the important correlation they reveal between God's requirement of our holiness and His desire for friendship.**
>
> **1 Chronicles 28:9**
>
> **Psalm 24:3-5**
>
> **2 Corinthians 6:14–7:1**
>
> **James 4:8-10**

"Depart, depart, go out from there, Touch nothing unclean; Go out of the midst of her, purify your-selves, You who carry the vessels of the LORD."
Isaiah 52:11

WHEN GOD COMES DOWN

God's appearance on the mountain was marked with specific terrifying manifestations that reminded all of the grandeur and greatness of God. If anyone had a casual view of Him before this day, it was about to change. Not only did they get to hear evidence of God's presence, they also got to see it.

> **Read Exodus 19:16-18. What did the people see when the Lord descended upon the mountain?**

> **What happened to the mountain when the Lord descended on it?**

> **How did the people respond to God's presence?**

In an effort to more fully reveal Himself to His people, God allowed proof of His presence to be seen. In fact, God's display of glory was so terrific that the people literally shook. Moses responded to the people's intense fear by encouraging them not to allow it to keep them from approaching and experiencing God. He said, "God has come … in order that the fear of Him may remain with you, so that you may not sin" (Ex. 20:20). While the people were allowing an unhealthy fear of God to keep them from intimacy with Him, Moses indicated a healthy reverence that should mark the believer's relationship with an awesome God.

> **When you encounter God's power, do you tend to run to Him or run away from Him? Why?**

The word *fear* appears twice in Exodus 20:20 during Moses' response to the people. Each time, the Hebrew root word for fear is the same: *yare*, but it's connotation is slightly different. *Yare* means "to fear, to be afraid, or to revere" and is an emotional reaction.[6] To clarify, one form of the verb indicates a terror that causes distance, and the other form refers to a reverence that inspires humility and worship. When Moses told the Israelites to "fear" God, he implied that a reverent and awe-inspiring view of God would keep them from making light of His covenant with them, thereby fostering appropriate intimacy. God didn't display His glory on the mountain so that they would run from Him but so that they would run to Him.

Consider the following verses. Underline the portions that reveal the benefit of having a healthy fear of God.

"The friendship of the Lord is for those who fear him, and he makes known to them his covenant." Psalm 25:14, ESV

"In that day he will be your sure foundation, providing a rich store of salvation, wisdom, and knowledge. The fear of the Lord will be your treasure." Isaiah 33:6, NLT

What false biblical teaching or world viewpoints foster an unhealthy fear of God?

Did you grow up in an environment that contributed to an unhealthy fear of God? If so, explain.

As we encounter God more fully and He allows us to see Him moving in our lives we can either run from God or run to Him. Remember, intimacy is His goal. So as you walk through this portion of your wilderness journey and press into Him by camping at the mountain of God, He desires to call you to Himself. He wants you to see Him in all of His splendor and glory. As you go through this study and continue to see Him in the Word and in your circumstances, you will most assuredly be astounded by His goodness, power, and holiness. The more clearly God comes into view, the more fully humbled and in awe of Him you should grow. Fearing God appropriately will foster a beautiful, vibrant relationship between your heart and His and that is what this journey is all about.

1. John L. Mackay. *Exodus* (Fearn, Ross-Shire, England: Mentor, 2001), 326, quoted in Philip Graham Ryken, *Exodus: Saved for God's Glory* (Wheaton, IL: Crossway Books, 2005), 494.
2. H.L. Willmington. Willmington's Book of Bible Lists (Wheaton, IL: Tyndale House, 1987), 92.
3. Merrill F. Unger. *The New Unger's Bible Dictionary* (Chicago: Moody, 1988), 259.
4. Liz Curtis Higgs. *Embrace Grace: Welcome to the Forgiven Life* (Colorado Springs: WaterBrook Press, 2006), 46.
5. J. Scott Horrell. *The Trinity: Father, Son and Holy Spirit* (Dallas: Dallas Theological Seminary, 2000), notes on Systematic Theology 402B, Spring 2000.
6. R. Laird Harris, ed. *Theological Wordbook of the Old Testament*, Vol. 1 (Chicago: Moody Press, 1980), 907–09.

Session 5
Viewer Guide

You can't do what you've _always_ _done_ and _expect_ _different_ _results_.

If we want to move on to promised land living, we have to start doing things differently.

John 10:10
"The thief comes only to steal and kill and destroy;
I came that they may have life, and have it abundantly."

The only two who made the trip to the promised land were _Joshua_ and _Caleb_.

They were willing to do things differently.

For _38_ _years_ they traveled in a circle around Kadesh-barnea.

The wilderness is not a _barrier_ to the promised land; _wandering_ in the wilderness is the barrier to the promised land.

Kadesh-Barnea was an oasis, the _oasis_ _of_ _complacency_

You know you are in the oasis of complacency when:

1. The promised land starts looking way _too_ _risky_.

2. You start feeling like you _have_ _arrived_.

3. The _enemy_ _stops_ trying to hinder your
progress.

[handwritten note: stop bringing for more]

"Nevertheless" *[handwritten: There was proof, but didn't accept it and said, "nevertheless"]*

[handwritten note in box: if enemy isn't distracting you — you are not a threat]

The people _saw_ and _still chose_ not to believe.

Numbers 13:23

"Then they came to the valley of Eshcol and from there cut down a branch with a single cluster of grapes; and they carried it on a pole between two men, with some of the pomegranates and the figs."

The spies had proof of God's ability, a "cluster" of proof.

What kind of _influencers (friends) spies_ do you have in your life?

[handwritten: God gave me evidence and I still say never the less]

What kind of influencer are you?

[handwritten: stands beside others in small group - help to instill desire for fullness of God]

Romans 8:19, "The anxious longing of the creation waits eagerly for the revealing of the sons of God."

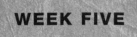

BREAKING BARRIERS

Trapeze artists are incredible performers. I've often stood in wide-eyed wonder over their courageous mid-air leaps from one tiny swinging bar to another. When they release their grip, they do so with the knowledge that another awaits their grasp. These incredible air-traveling acrobats grow comfortable with letting go because someone trustworthy makes certain that another sturdy bar arrives at just the right time.

Like the trapeze artists, you and I can let go and move on with confidence. Because the Lord will never leave us without the bar of His spiritual protection and the safety net of His grace, we can travel through life with the assurance that He will always send exactly what we need just when we need it.

Day 1
Changing Places

We've done a lot of work together, haven't we? For four weeks we've dug into the Scriptures to learn and digest details surrounding the Hebrews' exodus and wilderness wanderings. You've examined the contents of both your workbook as well as your own heart. We want to meditate on these Scriptures and process the powerful story of redemption to open ourselves up to a major soul overhaul. God is doing a work in us.

Take a deep breath. Let the tension ease out of your muscles. No matter how difficult, frustrating, or exhilarating you've found the journey so far, a shift is on the horizon. Today a new dimension of our study unfolds. In the first video I mentioned the three categories of our study. Week 1 we considered deliverance. Weeks 2–4 covered development. Weeks 5–6 we'll see destiny.

"The LORD our God spoke to us at Horeb, saying, 'You have stayed long enough at this mountain. Turn and set your journey, and go to the hill country of the Amorites … the land of the Canaanites, and Lebanon, as far as the great river, the river Euphrates.' "
Deuteronomy 1:6-7

From what were the Israelites delivered?
Pharoah. Egypt.

From what has God delivered you?
oppressions, grasp of sin

How did the wilderness develop the Hebrews?

Name two ways the wilderness has developed you.
1. *trust Him more*
2. *intimate relationship*

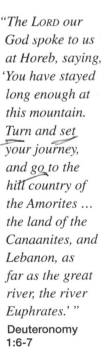

How does the term destiny correspond to Canaan?

According to John 10:10, what is your destiny as a Christ follower?

abundant life *joy in neediest of sorrow*

BREAKING CAMP

Three months after leaving Egypt, Israel arrived at Sinai, where they remained for about a year. After that pause in their travels, they made one last major geographical move to position them for the destiny God had long ago purposed for them.

Read Deuteronomy 1:2. Turn to your map and draw an arrow going around in a circle from Kadesh up toward the Jordan River and back.

Kadesh-barnea was in a larger area called the wilderness of Paran. This area became the Hebrews' camping site for the next 38 years. This land of transition bordered Canaan; there God positioned the Israelites for a major shift in their journey and prepped them for the promised land. Yahweh tested the Hebrews' true levels of faith and obedience at Kadesh-barnea, drastically impacting their future. Ultimately they would be required to leave behind Moses' model of leadership for a new way of thinking and acting to reach their destination.

While at the Jordan River on the border of Canaan Moses' sermon series reminded the people of where they began and what God had done prior to that point. First, he reminded the people of God's instructions that had brought them to this location on the edge of Canaan.

Look at Deuteronomy 1:6-7 at the beginning of today's lesson. Underline the three action verbs God used to direct the Hebrews.

Moses reminded the Israelites that God had given these three commands at Sinai. After a year of basking in the glow of God's magnificent presence, getting closer to Canaan would mean leaving familiar comforts. More importantly, it required the nomads to thoughtfully and deliberately calculate a travel plan. Destiny lay just over the horizon. Change was indeed coming. Following God's instructions was of utmost importance.

The verbs you underlined in Deuteronomy 1 are commands, not passive directives; they demanded a mobile response from all. That response required activity of minds, bodies, and spirits.

> Put yourself in the Israelites' sandals. Which fits your attitude toward breaking camp and moving forward?
> ▓ I'd rather stay where I feel safe. I don't like change.
> ▓ Here we go again. Wonder what God's got in store for us this time?
> ▓ Yes! Finally, I'm moving closer to the promised land!

> On page 88 you wrote what it would be like for you to camp at the mountain of God. What would it look like for you to break camp and move forward?

In our walks with the Lord, we too will discover moments when a season of camping out in the foothills of Sinai ends and we are compelled to take what we've gathered and move forward. When our souls begin to stir and the Holy Spirit begins gently nudging us to turn, set a new journey, and go, we can know that God is moving us to a new place in our relationship with Him.

> Describe a time when you felt the Lord prompting you to "turn, set a new journey, and go." How did you respond? What did you gain by obediently following His commands?

TAKING A TURN

Motherhood requires drastic physical and emotional changes. When my first child arrived, I thought that I could continue with life as usual while still earning my Super Mom cape. The footloose, fancy-free schedule that had governed my days turned joy over my son's arrival into massive frustration with life. My need for spontaneity disrupted much-needed naps for the little one, and my lack of attention to detail caused me to waste large quantities of time looking for misplaced things instead of bonding with my baby. After six months I was so tired, overwhelmed, and dissatisfied with the season of life that I didn't know what to do.

One of my beautiful, godly mentors stepped in to get me back on track. She lovingly but sternly said the mothering difficulties I faced weren't really about parenting as much as about a life-shift. God wanted to use motherhood and sensitivity to our family's needs to help me reprioritize and move forward with Him. Surrendering to this new season of life would allow me to align myself with the new direction He was steering me in spiritually.

Successful and sane motherhood required a turn from the way I'd been living, a deliberate calculation in the journey ahead, and a decision to act in conjunction with the new goals set before me. What worked in my life before no longer cut it. If I chose not to cooperate within a new set of parameters, I would continue in frustration as I missed the joy in this season of life and potentially delay the new things God had for me.

Closely following God to abundant living requires change in the life of every believer. We must turn away from the way we have lived, set our journeys according to the new paths God maps for us, and then go as He leads.

Read the following passages and briefly describe how each illustrates the three principles of turn, set your journey, and go.

"Since we have so great a cloud of witnesses surrounding us, let us also lay aside every encumbrance and the sin which so easily entangles us, and let us run with endurance the race that is set before us, fixing our eyes on Jesus, the author and perfecter of faith, who for the joy set before Him endured the cross, despising the shame, and has sat down at the right hand of the throne of God" (Heb. 12:1-2).

Turn:

Set Your Journey:

Go:

"Do you not know that those who run in a race all run, but only one receives the prize? Run in such a way that you may win. Everyone who competes in the games exercises self-control in all things. They then do it to receive a perishable wreath, but we an imperishable. Therefore I run in such a way, as not without aim; I box in such a way, as not beating the air; but I discipline my body and make it my slave, so that, after I have preached to others, I myself will not be disqualified" (1 Cor. 9:24-27).

Turn:

Set Your Journey:

Go:

Now consider your own life. From what is the Lord asking you to turn recently?

To what does He want you to chart a new course?

Briefly calculate the changes you may need to make in order to embrace His new journey for you. In the margin write about how you can move forward.

God's gifts require lifestyle modification to handle, enjoy, and fully appreciate them. In my transition into motherhood, the most difficult thing for me to do was to turn away from one way of living and to another. I'd grown comfortable in life without children. But as long as I rebelled against what the new season of life required, I felt agitated and unable to relax into God's journey for me. Only when I made the decision to turn and chart out a plan of action did motherhood, God's new place for my life, become a joy

God's gifts require lifestyle modification to handle, enjoy, and fully appreciate them.

Consider your answers in the last activity. What comforts in your current position (if any) might make the decision to turn seem difficult?

contentment

Which aspect of your calculated journey do you most anticipate? dread?

What can you do today to go with God?

change my heart to align to His will

God positioned Israel to a new stage of development. He took them to a location designed to focus their thoughts on their destiny as His children. They would face dynamic actions and life-changing decisions, each purposed to better align their hearts with His plans. Are you willing to embrace the something new the Lord wants to do in your life? If so, know that your destiny of abundance is waiting.

Turn from that rope ladder, grasp that trapeze bar, set your eyes on the platform ahead, and prepare to let go. My Sister, the Lord won't leave you dangling. He'll provide just what you need just when you need Him. Trust that He'll take care of you as you follow His new direction for your life.

Day 2
The Winds of Change

Feel the winds of change blowing? I love to feel the breeze of God's Spirit rustling the leaves of my soul. It always makes me a tad nervous because I know that change requires another area of surrender, but I always excitedly anticipate the next phase of my journey with God.

In 2004 my heart began burning in daily anticipation as I sensed His call to something new. I spent considerable time on my face before Him seeking clarity in His direction. I knew He was asking me to depend on Him more in ministry—specifically by trusting His direction in what I should teach when giving a message.

"Then Moses said to Hobab the son of Reuel the Midianite, Moses' father-in-law, 'We are setting out to the place of which the LORD said, "I will give it to you"; come with us and we will do you good, for the LORD has promised good concerning Israel.' "

Numbers 10:29

Within months, a women's group asked me to speak to them. I accepted the event because I believed it was a part of what God was doing in my life, though I wasn't exactly sure what that meant at the time. I did my usual planning, note-taking, praying, and prepping; but right before I walked on stage, I felt the Holy Spirit prompting a change in my plans. "Teach about the woman caught in adultery, Priscilla. Focus on the grace Jesus extended to her." I hadn't planned on teaching that. Didn't the Lord know that my notes were filled with information on an entirely different topic? I let out a nervous sigh and hesitantly agreed. In this very specific way, He was asking me to turn from my normal way of doing ministry, calculate a new way, and move forward in obedience. A shiver crawled up my spine as I made my way to the front.

The following week I received a letter from a woman who'd attended the event. She said that the day before I spoke, her involvement in an illicit affair became public. Even as the woman faced the possibility of losing her husband of 20 years and the family they'd made together, she found herself drawn to the conference. "There," she wrote, "I discovered that the Lord still loved me and cared enough about my situation to extend grace." This woman saw that the Lord had her on His mind when He laid that message on my heart.

God's Spirit led me into uncharted and uncomfortable territory that day, but He did so for a divine and wonderful purpose. Had I chosen to balk at the thought of embarrassing myself in front of those ladies, I would've missed a blessing that forever altered my life and my view of God.

Through what life circumstances has God confirmed that
He wants to do something new with you?

OBSTACLES TO DESTINY

When God spoke to Moses, the aging leader knew the Hebrews were headed
closer to the border of Canaan. Surely expectation came with the knowledge
that entry into the promised land was imminent. Moses readily embraced the
idea that God was doing something new, but he had concerns.

The Israelites' trek to the edge of destiny would not come without
difficulty. In Numbers 10 Moses chronicled the preparation steps and early
traveling notes of the Israelites' move into Kadesh-barnea.

**Which terms in Numbers 10:35-36 suggest that Moses
anticipated the journey to Canaan would prove difficult?**

Moses knew they were entering a land of opposition. Just because God said
this land is yours did not mean the local inhabitants would simply hand it to
them. The Hebrews were a threat to the Canaanites. The ancient world was
filled with enemies who knew well what God had done for His people in
delivering them from Egypt. They dreaded what He might do to any other
nations who opposed them. Undoubtedly, the Hebrews' forward movement
sent many men to sharpen their swords and contemplate methods of attack.

Above all else, our enemy the Devil hates Christians who intend to enter
new territory with God. We, like Moses, must anticipate our Enemy's desire
to thwart our progress as we move toward God's plan for us. He's not going
to just hand it to us. We are going to have to fight for it. The Devil and his
troops will seek to intimidate, discourage, and dissuade us from our mission
to become more like Christ. We cannot allow complacency or a false sense
of security to numb us to Satan's advances. Complacency is his most valued
position for the Christian. So he uses fear and doubt as tools to keep us from
moving into new spiritual territory.

*"Finally, be
strong in the
Lord and in the
strength of His
might. Put on
the full armor
of God, so that
you will be
able to stand
firm against
the schemes
of the devil."*
Ephesians 6:10-11

**What battle strategies does the Enemy use to keep you
from walking forward with God? Circle your answers.**

fear   feelings of inadequacy   sin

complacency   guilt   people-pleasing

other: _____

For each one you circled, read the passages that serve as defensive weapons against the Enemy's attacks.

Fear: *2 Timothy 1:7*
Feelings of inadequacy: *2 Corinthians 3:5-6*
Sin: *1 Peter 5:8-9; 1 John 1:9*
Complacency: *Ephesians 5:14-16; Revelation 3:15-20*
Guilt: *Romans 8:1*
People-pleasing: *Colossians 1:10; 1 Thessalonians 2:4*

Choose your favorite verse and write it on a card. Memorize it and recite it aloud the next time the Devil tries to discourage you in your journey with the Lord.

PREPARED FOR BATTLE

I love that even as Moses' words warned of battle, he spoke in the assurance of victory.

"Then it came about when the ark set out that Moses said, 'Rise up, O LORD! And let Your enemies be scattered, And let those who hate You flee before You.' "
Numbers 10:35

In what did Moses place confidence? (Num. 10:35).
▨ **his ability to wield a staff**
▨ **the people's willingness to fight**
✓ **the Lord's presence**
▨ **the military ineptitude of the local nations**

Moses knew success against any enemy was guaranteed only if God's presence remained exalted among His obedient people. He voiced his thoughts in Exodus 33:15,16: "[God,] if Your presence does not go with us, do not lead us up from here. ... that we ... may be distinguished from all the other people who are upon the face of the earth." Moses realized that without the Lord's continuous protective guidance, the people could never stand against opposition of any sort. They could not begin to cherish intimacy with God at Sinai and then throw His presence aside as they left the mountain. Yes, the people must move onward, but they must move onward with God!

Often our tendency is to experience God in one portion of our journey and then think we can move forward without Him. No one can move ahead spiritually (or in the Israelites' case, physically) without continued connection with God. The fellowship and faith we garner in the wilderness at the mountain of God are designed to keep our eyes on the Lord and to help us trust in His plans. We must daily seek fellowship with Him.

What about your life makes it difficult to keep ongoing connection with God?

I have a file recording God's voice and activity during a time when God was wooing me to Himself in a more intimate way. When I sensed Him calling me to turn from one way of living to another, I found I tended to run ahead on the momentum of all He had been doing. Before I knew it, my quiet time began to wane and my file became less filled with evidence of God's presence.

    I became more focused on the journey than on the One who called me to it. My tendency to be task-oriented caused me to look to "the next thing" rather than prioritize relationship with Him. I found myself being drawn away from the reason I'd spent so much time at Sinai with God—to know Him more intimately and focus my attention on Him for the remainder of my journey.

Special Assignment: In your group this week, discuss creative and practical ways that fellowship with God can be continued during this season in your life.

In the margin, would you describe yourself as a task-oriented person? ▇ yes ▇ no If so, what current tasks take your attention away from relationship with God?

FRUSTRATED WITH GOD

According to Numbers 11:1, how did Israel react to the knowledge that their journey might come with difficulty?

Does your reaction to adversity sometimes mirror that of the Israelites? ▇ yes ▇ no How do you think your actions make God feel?

"Now the people became like those who complain of adversity in the hearing of the LORD; and when the LORD heard it, His anger was kindled, and the fire of the LORD burned among them and consumed some of the outskirts of the camp."
Numbers 11:1

You'd think that after such an extended period of time daily experiencing God's presence at Sinai, they might confidently trust in God's ability to protect. Yet the knowledge that enemies and obstacles still stood between them and Canaan left the people discouraged and frustrated.

    A close friend's life seems filled with heartache. I hurt that God would ask her to endure so much. Her wish to come home from full-time work so that she could spend time with her daughter was answered after years of prayer. Soon after that, however, she was diagnosed with rheumatoid arthritis and now lives under its crippling effects. On the heels of this news, my friend discovered her husband's affair and his desire to leave their family. His infidelity forced her to look for a new job, and the pressures of life weighed heavily.

Not surprisingly, this sister is a bit tired of girding for the battle each day. Yet in the midst of all she endures, she exudes an overwhelming sense of peace, joy, and strength. Never does a conversation fail to revolve around her complete trust in the Master's care despite her discomfort. As a result, the Lord is lovingly holding her hand as she navigates over and around every difficulty.

How do you react when it seems that your journey, although moving forward, will still encounter difficulty?

How do you feel when you see this in the lives of others who seem to be faithfully following God?

Sister, despite the difficulties you will inevitably face as you follow God's plan for you, keep God's presence exalted. Don't become complacent and don't give in to fear. Trust that God is with you. I promise you'll discover—just as my friend and Moses did—that the Lord is enough.

Day 3
Window Shopping

Yesterday my family ate at one of our favorite restaurants, an eatery famous for its amazing viewing case full of tantalizing desserts. Even as we entered, my mouth watered for the Lemon Extravaganza, a lemon pound cake drenched in lemon sauce and flanked by ice cream, strawberries, and a huge dollop of homemade whipped cream. On the way to our table, I smiled as we passed a big piece of it on display.

You can imagine my devastation when the waiter told me that the menu had undergone an overhaul, resulting in my favorite dessert's deletion. When I mentioned the display slice, he commented that it was a leftover and not available for sale. Nothing feels quite like seeing and then being denied your heart's desire.

By the time God led Moses to Nebo, the summit of Mount Pisgah, he had survived one generation of wilderness wanderers. When he stood on this peak, just opposite Jericho, he had a clear view of the first city the Israelites would conquer when entering the promised land. Beyond Jericho lay a panoramic view of Canaan. Deuteronomy 34:1-2 explains that from that vantage point, Moses had a view of Gilead as far as Dan as well as the land of Naphtali, Ephraim, and Manasseh. The entirety of Judah as far as the Mediterranean Sea, the Negev, and the plain in the valley of Jericho met his eyes.

From that perspective, he could see the four major marks of the Hebrews' future inheritance. Between 50 and 60 miles of God's promised territory lay before him! Moses got a look at the entire dessert case, yet neither he nor the vast majority of the Israelites would ever be able to enter and experience it.

> **Turn to your map and draw a magnifying glass in the position where Moses looked out over Canaan.**

What emotions do you think Moses experienced while viewing the promised land? Have you ever felt that promised-land living was just for you to view and not for you to experience?

"Then the Lord said to him, 'This is the land which I swore to Abraham, Isaac, and Jacob, saying, "I will give it to your descendants"; I have let you see it with your eyes, but you shall not go over there.' "
Deuteronomy 34:4

WHAT TO DO WHEN CANAAN'S IN VIEW

My parents didn't negotiate Sunday morning church attendance with their children. I jokingly claim that in our household the only legitimate excuse for missing church was if my body was rolled down the aisle in a casket. My parents would be satisfied because at least part of me would still be there!

In my youth, I often sat through lively testimonial services where seasoned saints shared their experiences with God. As I sat in rapt attention, they'd talk about experiencing His power, walking in His fruit and gifts and living as overcomers during trying circumstances. By college, I became frustratingly aware that my Christian life was bland and lacking compared with many in our congregation. When I heard them thanking God for His obvious presence and favor, I inwardly squirmed while simultaneously applauding God's work for them. I felt like a spiritual window-shopper, who only saw God's activity from afar but who had yet to experience Him in a personal way.

Every time I saw the hope and joy in the eyes of those sweet saints, I longed to draw closer to God and encounter Him as they had. I saw the promise of abundant life in their faces.

> **Whose relationship with the Lord do you admire? Why? In what specific ways has that person's experience with God affected your relationship with Him?**

I'm convinced God often gives us a view of Canaan through the lives of other believers so that we might long for spiritual milk and honey ourselves. Sadly, some believers see the abundant life expressed in the lives of others yet never press on to promised-land living for themselves. To me, spiritual "window shopping" reflects the most unsatisfying Christian experience of all.

We can imagine the elation that surely filled Moses' heart as he looked out over Canaan. Unfortunately, the moment was shrouded by sadness as he was in essence told "Look but don't touch."

Read Numbers 20:8-12. How did Moses offend the Lord?

Why do you think the Lord withheld entry into Canaan rather than assigning a lesser punishment?

What may seem minor disobedience to us was actually a sign of unbelief in God's ability as well as a defamation of God's character. Israel and its leader were marked by rebellion, disobedience, and unbelief—earmarks proving them unworthy of Canaan. Those same traits will keep us from walking in the full measure of freedom and abundance that Christ offers as well.

From the preceeding paragraph complete the following:
Disobedience is really a sign of _____.
Disobedience defames _____.

"Do not regard lightly the discipline of the Lord, nor faint when you are reproved by Him. For those whom the Lord loves He disciplines and He scourges every son who He receives."
Hebrews 12:5-6

A look at Deuteronomy 28:1-2 (NIV) further explains God's harsh punishment for Moses' disobedience: "If you *fully* obey the LORD your God and *carefully* follow all his commands I give you today, the LORD your God will set you high above all the nations on earth. All these blessings will come upon you and accompany you if you obey the LORD your God" (my emphasis added).

Why do you think God priced obedience so highly?

Canaan was promised to Israel, but only an obedient and believing generation would see that promise fulfilled. Moses' lack of total obedience kept him from walking Canaan's fertile soil.

When rebellion against God marks our lives, it shows our lack of trust in Him. If we don't believe Him, we won't fully commit to obedience. We'll never experience the abundant life He's promised. Lack of faith stops the believer's journey with God at the edge of the promised land. We must take doing what the Lord says seriously and trust Him. We can't ignore His Word.

The first two lessons this week, you wrote specific ways the Lord has asked you to "turn, set your journey, and go." Are you refusing to obey any part of this instruction? If so, in the margin record the reasons why.

I've spent too much of my spiritual journey seeing but not experiencing. I've stood on the parameters of others' lives as God blessed them with spiritual plenty while leaving me with spiritual boredom. Today, praise God, I'm dissatisfied with just viewing milk and honey. I want to taste it for myself. If I want to experience all God has for me, then obedience is the key.

"The thief comes only to steal and kill and destroy; I came that they may have life, and have it abundantly."
John 10:10

ENHANCE OUR VISION

God showed Moses the whole land of Canaan (Deut. 34:1-2). The sight required divine assistance. One commentator said this was not an ecstatic vision, "but a sight with the bodily eyes, whose natural power of vision was miraculously increased by God, to give Moses a glimpse … of the glorious land … the inheritance intended for his people."[1] God apparently granted Moses divine sight to better view the blessings ahead. I believe He did this so Moses would (1) develop a deeper appreciation for God's provision, (2) truly long for the fulfillment of God's promise, (3) and recognize the tragedy of missing out on the promised land's blessings.

"Lord, enhance our vision!" That is my prayer for us. I desire with my whole heart for God to grant us divine sight as the eyes of our hearts seek the land of abundant life. I don't want us to just see the words of Scripture as we open our Bibles; my hope is that we'll have a deep revelation of God's personal messages for us.

As I weave through life's frustrations and joys, I desire to really see God's activity and to recognize His invitations to join in His work. I want to be sensitive to the Spirit's prompting. I want to more fully see the breadth and height of the abundant life God has for me. This type of spiritual sight requires the Lord showing us all of the spiritual territory He has for us by the Spirit's power and then giving us to the desire and courage to go after it with all of our might.

Paul desired this same thing for those with whom he shared the gospel. To conclude today's lesson, read Ephesians 1:17-20 and then personalize it as a prayer to the Lord.

An Invitation for All

One of only two African-American girls in my gymnastics class, I began the season fairly naïve to the racial divide that existed in our group. As a result, I was shocked to find myself often ignored and chosen as the class laughingstock.

I will never forget when one of my teammates invited "everyone" to her house for a birthday slumber party. "Your individual invitations," she said with a smile, "are in your lockers."

At the end of that day's intense workout, we went to our locker room where each girl giggled as she took out her invitation. As their excitement echoed through the room, I dug underneath my sweat suit, around my water bottle, and under my grips. Nothing. I hadn't been accidentally forgotten; I really wasn't invited.

The Book of Deuteronomy opens with what appears an insignificant statement. Notice to whom Moses spoke (Deut 1:1). God's words were to every person in Israel. His invitation to experience the milk and honey of Canaan was not for a select few but for the entire group redeemed from Egypt. And unlike the little girl in my gymnastics group, God stays true to His word.

Despite their personal shortcomings and past mistakes, every Hebrew was extended the same opportunity: obey God and reap the rewards. God's invitation to promised-land living was not only for Israel's leadership, priests, judges, or Levitical servants, it was also for the regular men and women who lived and worked within the camp.

I can't begin to tell you how many times I, a regular woman, have felt as if God's promises were not for me, as if His invitation to abundant life made it into every locker but mine. My favorite Bible teacher, those serving at my church, and older people with a long godly legacy—I thought those were the only people God invited to experience Him abundantly. I lived under the belief that past decisions and choices I'd made, sins I'd committed, and plain old seasons of rebellion against God forever exempted me from abundant life. As I wallowed in self-defeat, I missed a critical piece of good news.

Listen to Jesus " 'I am the bread of life. [Everyone] who comes to me will never go hungry, and [everyone] who believes in me will never be thirsty. All that the Father gives me will come to me, and whoever comes to me I will never drive away'" (John 6:35,37 NIV). God's invitation to eat at His table and live in His grace belongs to all who accept it!

"These are the words which Moses spoke to all Israel across the Jordan in the wilderness, in the Arabah opposite Suph, between Paran and Tophel and Laban and Hazeroth and Dizahab."
Deuteronomy 1:1

Have you ever felt exempt from:

- seeing God's activity
- hearing God's voice
- exercising God's gifts
- exhibiting God's fruit
- experiencing His presence
- experiencing God's power
- walking by His Spirit
- receiving God's grace

If you checked any, record the reason why.

For each of the selections you made above, circle the passage showing God's invitation for you. Then rewrite in one sentence the main point of the verse you choose.

His presence—John 14:16-17; 2 Corinthians 6:16
His activity—Mark 5:25-29; John 5:17; 1 Peter 3:18
His voice—John 8:47a; 10:27; 14:26
His Spirit—Romans 8:9-11; John 14:26
His gifts   1 Corinthians 12
His fruit—Galatians 5:16-18,22-23
His grace—Hebrews 4:16; 2 Corinthians 9:8

Choose one of the following biblical illustrations and answer the corresponding questions in the margin.

Rahab—Joshua 2
1. What distinguishing characteristics of Rahab from verse 1 appear to exclude her from Israel's salvation?
2. How does God's grace being extended to her reveal His grace extended to you?

The Prodigal Son—Luke 15:11-31
1. How would you describe the son's lifestyle choices?
2. How would you react if this were one of your children?
3. How did the son feel when he returned to his father?
4. How did the father respond to the son's return?

In what ways does your life mirror the character you just studied?

"The mystery is that people who have never heard of God and those who have heard of him all their lives (what I've been calling outsiders and insiders) stand on the same ground before God. They get the same offer, same help, same promises in Christ Jesus. The Message is accessible and welcoming to everyone, across the board."
Ephesians 3:6,
THE MESSAGE

119

*"If our gospel
is veiled, it is
veiled to those
who are perish-
ing, in whose
case the god
of this world
has blinded
the minds of
the unbeliev-
ing so that they
might not see
the light of the
gospel of the
glory of Christ,
who is the
image of God."*
2 Corinthians
4:3-4

THE ENEMY'S PLOY

Our enemy, the Devil, stands behind any feelings that make us consider ourselves outsiders uninvited to a life of relationship with God. Remember, while Christ offers abundant life to us, the Enemy will do everything he can to steal, kill, and destroy its possibility in our lives (John 10:10).

Second Corinthians 4:3-4 sends a chill of holy anger down my spine. Satan blinds people's minds so they can't see the light of the gospel. If the Enemy blinds the eyes of those who are not saved, then it only stands to reason that he is also behind the blinded eyes of those who are. Satan's goal is to keep believers from fully recognizing all that their relationship with Christ can offer them. That is why Paul prayed so fervently that "the eyes of your heart may be enlightened, so that you will know … the riches of the glory of His inheritance" (Eph. 1:18). I know you've seen an example of how Satan has blinded the mind of an unsaved person so they can't understand the grace of Christ.

Who was this person and how was it obvious that the Enemy was behind their blindness?

How do you feel about Satan having an organized plan to keep people from their spiritual destiny?
■ **I'm angry that the Enemy has a plan against me.**
■ **I think I need an equally organized plan to combat this.**
■ **Satan has nothing to do with it. We keep ourselves from recognizing and experiencing God's plan.**

How have you personally experienced Satan's plan to make you feel distant from and unworthy of your inheritance as a believer?

INVITATION REVOKED?

Many skeptics of the biblical story struggle with the fact that God barred Moses as well as thousands of other Israelites from entering the land He'd promised. Some say this action demonstrates a weakness in God's character, suggesting He is quick to retract His promises when people don't behave as He'd like. Remember, Israel repeatedly aroused Yahweh's anger because of their blatant rebellion. As a direct result, the vast majority of those who wandered the desert never set foot in Canaan, but that didn't mean that God's love for them dimmed or even that He'd changed His mind.

God doesn't revoke invitations to a dynamic relationship with Himself. We must consider Israel's story in its greater context. According to the conditions of the covenant the Lord made with them, the Hebrews had to walk in continued obedience to receive benefit.

Thousands of years after Moses, God sent an open invitation to the world: "Believe that My Son Jesus took on your sins, ask for His forgiveness, and then receive abundant life and a heavenly inheritance!" Whether you have a tainted past like Rahab or have wandered from the Father like the prodigal son, God still offers you full access to the abundant life. Have you known an unlikely Christian, a man or woman with a past or situation so colorful that their decision to follow Christ is an obvious miracle?

How does that person's testimony affect how you view your own relationship with God?

All people, from those who've never heard of God to those who have heard about Him all their lives, stand on the same ground before God. They get the same offer and the same promises in Christ Jesus. God's invitation is accessible and welcoming to everyone. While the Enemy can't nullify believers' acceptance of Christ, he'll do everything he can to make them feel as if their invitation to abundance is revoked.

REST FOR ALL

Hebrews chapter 4 encourages believers with a promise of rest that clearly parallels Israel's inheritance of Canaan. Moses described the promised land as the place of their rest (Deut. 12:9-11; 31:18-20). The invitation to the Hebrews redeemed from the shackles of Egypt still stands for those redeemed from the shackles of sin through Christ.

Now and for all eternity, believers can live—not without trouble but without anxiety and fear. We can rest in the experiential guidance of a loving Father. The question is not whether we've been offered this invitation but whether we will accept it and take part in the abundant rest that He has offered us.

You and I must individually decide to follow God's rules if we want to take full advantage of His invitation. But make no mistake about it, my friend; you are invited to participate in active, ongoing relationship with God. No matter what you have done the invitation has not been revoked. Open up the "locker" of His written Word and you'll find your golden-sealed invitation tucked inside. Treasure it, accept it, and get busy living by it.

"Therefore, let us fear if, while a promise remains of entering His rest, any one of you may seem to have come short of it. … For we who have believed enter that rest, just as He has said."
Hebrews 4:1,3

Day 5
Mourn and Move On

> *"So the sons of Israel wept for Moses in the plains of Moab thirty days; then the days of weeping and mourning for Moses came to an end."*
>
> **Deuteronomy 34:8**

A major shift is about to occur for the Hebrews. Deuteronomy 34:7-8 explains that Moses died at 120 years of age. Surely this loss came as a huge blow to the people who'd counted on his leadership throughout the last several decades. Moses was not just a man who gave them directions; he also embodied their hope for Canaan. How many times had he been the mediator between them and the wrath of God? How many times had their journey been made easier because God used Moses as a tool for a miracle? The people surely wondered whether continued victory could be achieved without Moses' guidance.

Since God would not allow Moses to enter Canaan, the people could not move ahead under his leadership. While the loss of this cherished leader led to heavy mourning, the Israelites had to remain determined to press onward. There was new ground to cover and 40 years had already been lost. Had they allowed sadness to discourage them, they would have missed out on the exciting new chapter in God's plans for them as He raised a new leader, Joshua, to take the people into their new home.

As we go to new dimensions in our relationships with the Lord, God often asks us to embrace a new phase of the journey that sometimes requires that we leave behind the familiar to embrace the new. While such steps are often painful, each is necessary if our spiritual growth is to continue unhindered.

What has God asked you to relinquish as you journey on with Him? From the list in the margin, circle all that apply. Star the two with which you have the most difficulty.

How did you cope with those losses?

a person

a relationship

an ambition

a life goal

a habit

a lifestyle choice

a religious comfort zone

control of your time

other

Briefly explain the danger of not letting go of the things God asks us to give up.

Though the loss in our story regards the death of a person, our purpose is to see how the biblical event applies to us. As we grieve the loss of things that hinder our relationships with God, we must take care not to allow our laments to blind us to the new thing God wants to do for and through us.

Remember my transition into motherhood? Leaving behind the life I'd known left me grieving for the joys of singleness. While my tears seem silly to me now as I've grown into mothering and fallen helplessly in love with my babies, I recognize that the sadness and despondency I felt at the time could've derailed me from the things the Lord had in store. Had I clung to my frustration over what I'd lost, I would've missed God's exciting new mission for me.

Handling the death of the things and relationships takes effort, however. A healthy response to these losses hinges on what I call the Principle of Mourning and Moving On. Expressing grief or sorrow is always the starting place when we face a hurt. Whether we've lost a friend, relinquished a job, or even said good-bye to a long-time, comforting habit, we need time to mourn.

Some Christian groups discourage people from embracing sad or distressing feelings, dismissing them as a sign of spiritual weakness. Instead of allowing time for a believer to talk through and express emotion over a loss, these groups encourage the hurting to "just get on with life."

Don't buy into such a mentality. Scripture says, "Rejoice with them that do rejoice, and weep with them that weep" (Rom. 12:15, KJV). The Bible clearly supports the idea that sometimes people need to grieve. Mourning is a healthy expression of sadness that assists us in moving on.

Did you grow up in an environment that encouraged expression of emotion, or one that dissuaded you from expressing emotion?

How has this affected you? Do you encourage expression of emotion by those around you or discourage it? Why?

In their work "Grief, Loss and Transition," the counselors at one prominent church teach that "we have three options for dealing with loss:
1. We may ignore (deny) the loss.
2. We may get lost in the loss cycle and replay the past over and over through what are called flashbacks.
3. We can resolve the loss and find new meaning in [a] relationship … [or thing] to [which we were] attached."[2]

While we should definitely take the time to mourn our losses, we must also come to accept them and use them as a springboard into the future.

Underline which of the three numbered points best describes how you deal with loss.

You've made or been challenged to make lots of difficult decisions during our study. The journey to abundance requires those types of choices. You've left Egypt and its comforts and traveled through a wilderness that is downright uncomfortable. Each time you move forward God has asked you to surrender something for the journey. Don't feel guilty about lamenting what you've let go of. Everyone mourns differently.

Some of us don't deal with our sadness at all while others mourn and then get over losses relatively quickly. Still others hang onto emotional distress far longer than is healthy. The children of Israel mourned for 30 days. The normal time of mourning was seven days, yet the gravity of what they were losing required more emotional healing.

Friend, will you allow me to give you permission to grieve what you've left behind and pray that godly mentors will help you move forward when the time is right? Remember, while "weeping may endure for a night, but joy comes in the morning" (Ps. 30:5, NKJV). Grief comes in seasons. Don't allow it to define your life.

MOVING ON

The customs of mourning in ancient times encouraged a very visual and vivid expression of grief. Some biblical mourners tore their clothes, dressed in sackcloth, sat in sprinkled ashes or dust, shaved their heads, cut their hair, fasted, or sat in long period of silence. Families that had enough money would even hire professional mourners to add their laments to the chants of the grieving family. The time dedicated to mourning a loss was filled with very deliberate actions designed to focus the mind back on the person lost.

How might a lengthy season of mourning prove harmful?

Mourning is healthy, but Scripture explains that while "[there is] a time to weep," there is also "a time to laugh … and a time to dance" (Eccl. 3:4). A month after their great leader passed, Israel's observance of deliberate cultural activities to lament were put aside. They had to choose not to participate in them anymore. This does not mean that their hearts were no longer saddened, but they made a choice to stop participating in traditional mourning activities and continue moving forward in the journey.

I must admit, not acting sad when I still feel sad is difficult. While I might enjoy the catharsis of mentally reliving the details of a loss, I must remain sensitive to the fact that doing so after an appropriate period of time can hinder me from moving forward in my journey with God.

In the chart below, record the specifics of two things the Lord has asked you to relinquish to move forward with Him. (Remember, you circled general topics in the beginning of the day.) Fill in the chart with appropriate information regarding each one. I've given an example.

What I Lost	How I Grieved	Difficult Actions to Stop	How Those Actions Hindered My Progress
I lost an important relationship.	I talked about it to friends and rehearsed hurt feelings in my mind.	Gossiping about it on the phone	Remembering the negative prevents me from realizing the benefits of new relationships.

Israel's decision to stop expending energy to focus on Moses' death proved beneficial to their future. As the echoes of their laments died, God raised up "Joshua, the son of Nun ... filled with the spirit of wisdom" (Deut. 34:9). Joshua's fearless leadership would soon lead Israel into the promised land.

The loss of your Moses may be difficult, but take courage; Joshua is coming! As we grieve those things that must die so that we can move more fully into the Spirit-filled, abundant life, let's remember that better things are on the horizon. Make a wise decision when to choose to stop the actions of mourning so that your heart can be encouraged and begin to heal. Lift up your head, my friend. God is up to something new and you won't want to miss it.

May God heal our hearts so that we can fully embrace the next leg of our journey.

1. Carl Friedrich Keil and Franz Delitzsch. *Commentary on the Old Testament* (Peabody, MA: Hendrickson, 2002), 1020.
2. Prestonwood Baptist Church. "Grief, Loss and Transition" (Plano, TX: Prestonwood Baptist Church, n.d.), 11.

Session 6
Viewer Guide

Moses had to _die_ before Joshua could become leader.

The time for mourning does come to an end— _act over it_.

Joshua 3:1
"Then Joshua rose early in the morning; and he and all the sons of Israel set out from Shittim and came to the Jordan, and they lodged there before they crossed."

1. Joshua _acted_ _immediately_ in obedience to God.

   The land of promise is often lost by _lingering_ or _procrastinating_.

   What do we miss because we don't obey immediately?

2. Joshua _acted_ _fearlessly_, in spite of insurmountable odds.

Joshua 3:1-2
"Then Joshua rose early in the morning; and he and all the sons of Israel set out from Shittim and came to the Jordan, and they lodged there before they crossed. At the end of three days the officers went through the midst of the camp."

Joshua took God at His _word_.

one
in a million

God doesn't call people because they are equipped. He
___equips___ them because He's ___called___ them.
The area of ___sensitivity___ and ___tenderness___
in your life is probably the area where God wants you to
experience the most victory, where He wants the biggest
ministry to come from your life.

God doesn't call us to do the possible. He calls us to do the
___impossible___ and then He equips us to handle it.

3. Joshua ___acknowledged___ the presence of God.

Joshua 3:3
**"They commanded the people, saying, 'When you see the ark
of the covenant of the LORD your God with the Levitical priests
carrying it, then you shall set out from your place and go after it.'"**

John 5:19
**"Jesus answered and was saying to them, 'Truly, truly, I say to
you, the Son can do nothing of Himself, unless it is something
He sees the Father doing; for whatever the Father does, these
things the Son also does in like manner.'"**

follow after God

Joshua 3:5
**"Then Joshua said to the people, 'Consecrate yourselves,
for tomorrow the LORD will do wonders among you.'"**

4. Joshua ___anticipate___ God's miracles all around him.

Start living today like God has already performed the biggest
miracle of your life.

Jesus only did the Fathers will and nothing else.

ASPIRING TO ABUNDANCE

Thousands of fish swim in the pond near our home. Many find themselves on a fisherman's hook, but an infamously large bass lurks untouched in the depths. Occasionally he'll surface as if to remind us he's there. Every time he's sighted, fishermen renew their efforts to catch him, often sitting for hours in hopes they'll reel him in.

Just this weekend I took my boys fishing at the pond; within an hour my three-year-old caught seven fish and my other son snagged four. No large bass for us, only sun perch. Even though I knew we had little hope of catching the legendary monster in the pond, I found myself peering out over the still dark waters with intensity. I couldn't help but wonder if the elusive bass would ever bite someone's hook.

In the days of Moses, millions of Jews swam in the grace and protection of Yahweh, yet the Lord quickly determined that few had a faith worth reeling in for the use of His greater purposes. A quick look within the depths of the tent-lined camps revealed that few people really believed God and fully expected the inheritance they'd been promised. But among the two million people who'd left Egypt with Canaan in mind, two men chose to keep trusting that God would provide just what He'd promised. Hear that again: Of approximately two million Hebrews, only two out of those held accountable would ever walk on Canaan's land.

The Israelites' new leader, Joshua, was truly one in a million.

Day 1
One in a Million

Just as the vast majority of Israelites failed to rely fully on God, many modern Christ followers fall short of placing full confidence in God's power and abilities. If only a handful of Christians really experience God, I want my name listed among those few. When God peers out over the waters of those swimming in His grace and love, I hope He'll find our names listed among those people ready and willing to take Him at His word, those who want to fully engage in the inheritance He has planned.

In our video lessons we've discussed what promised-land living looks like for modern believers. In the margin list facets of abundant life that stand out in your mind.

129

one
in a million

Why do you think
it is difficult to find
Christians who
really believe God
and expect to
experience all that
He has promised?

Among Christians you know, is it ▇ easy, ▇ somewhat easy, ▇ difficult, or ▇ very difficult to think of someone who is experiencing abundant life in Christ?

What similarities do you see among the people who are enjoying God's inheritance?

When I began to search the Scripture to see what my inheritance from God looks like, I was stunned to see how much more there was than I thought there would be. I noticed that I was leaving out promises that either I didn't know about or really didn't expect to experience.

Look at your Promised-Land Living list on page 160. Draw a plus sign beside the list items you fully expect to experience and a minus sign beside those you don't.

Since our goal is to expect God's best and march into our personal Canaan, we can start by considering why only two of the original Hebrews marched victoriously into theirs. By focusing on the characteristics of Joshua, we'll discover how to more fully realize the inheritance God intends for us.

Courage is the
attitude of fac-
ing ... anything
recognized as
dangerous, dif-
ficult, or painful
instead of with-
drawing from it.[1]

COURAGE TO COME WHEN CALLED

Joshua was chosen to lead the people into the promised land. This bold and valiant leader had arrived on the scene some 40 years before when he commanded Israel's war with the Amalekites. The very first time we encounter him, Joshua is being commissioned into national service.

Neither Moses' nor Joshua's background made them likely candidates for the roles God chose for them. Moses lived as a simple shepherd, yet God called him to lead people out of slavery; Joshua likely spent his early days as a slave making bricks. In both instances, the Lord enabled these faithful men to handle their assignments. Two men. Both called by God. Both sovereignly asked to lead without prior training. The similarities in their callings stop here.

Compare and contrast Joshua's and Moses' responses to God's call.

Joshua—Exodus 17:10

Moses—Exodus 3:11,13; 4:1,10

Throughout the past five weeks we've discussed the importance of obedience. Obviously this fundamental to the faith was very much a part of Joshua's response to his commission. Yet his quick acceptance showed more than just his willingness to obey; it pointed to an unwavering courage in the face of risk. This courage is the first clear difference between Joshua and Moses.

- One was unsure in himself and God's ability while the other never questioned either.
- One was concerned about who and what was against Him while the other looked immediately to One who was for him.
- One sought to escape the duty while the other faced it head on.

Courage is not the absence of fear. It is the will to move forward in spite of it.

Rather than grow unsure of himself and question God's ability, Joshua demonstrated complete confidence in the One who was on his side. Our very first encounter with Joshua reveals a man who courageously engaged in the tasks he was divinely called to encounter.

Prior to Exodus 17 we find no record of Joshua leading the people in any way. Yet when he was called without warning, Joshua didn't shrink back into his tent while pointing to someone more suited for the task; instead, he engaged in God's call and assumed the responsibility given him. Joshua believed God had equipped him. The result of his courage was a victorious win over a formidable foe (Ex. 17:13-14).

How did God respond to Moses' excuses? (Exodus 4:14).
☐ became angry   ☐ gave the job to Aaron instead
☐ banned the Israelites from the promised land

What does Joshua's lack of excuses reveal about his level of faith?

Has God called you to do something for which you are making excuses? If so, list it below. In the margin list the top three excuses you've been using.

What do excuses regarding why you can't do what God asks reveal about how you view yourself? How you view God?

For each of Moses' excuses, God had a response. God assured Moses that his inability could not override divine ability working through him. The same is true of every circumstance in a believer's life.

*"Be strong and
courageous, for
you shall give
this people
possession of
the land which
I swore to their
fathers to give
them. Only be
strong and very
courageous;
be careful to
do according
to all the law
which Moses
My servant
commanded you;
do not turn from
it to the right
or to the left, so
that you may
have success
wherever you go.
Do not tremble
or be dismayed,
for the LORD
your God is with
you wherever
you go."*

Joshua 1:6-7,9

LIVING COURAGEOUSLY

Joshua took the helm of leadership 38 years after the battle with the Amalekites. Often in His interaction with the new leader, God placed emphasis on one extremely important principle. Note God's command in the margin.

Taking Canaan would be no easy venture; however, it was completely possible for a man willing to obey God's calling with a holy confidence. Joshua's successful entry into the promised land hinged on his determination to remain courageous in his journey. Stepping into the abundant life of promised-land living takes courage. Remember, few of the Israelites shared Joshua's devotion to obey God's command to "be strong and courageous." Similarly, few of God's people will follow you to abundant life. The battles you'll fight and the unconventional means by which the Lord may ask you to fight them will require a firm commitment to do as God asks. We can't allow fear to creep in.

Why will a holy courage be necessary to complete the tasks God is calling you to right now?

As you begin to feel a divine tugging in your heart and explore spiritual abundance by opening your ears to God's voice and looking for the manifested presence of God around you be sure you will draw the Enemy's attention. The Devil will not wait patiently for you to acquire your God-given inheritance. He knows that once you enter the abundant life of Canaan you will never want to leave. His goal is to scare you off before your palate can grow accustomed to the taste of milk and honey. With this in mind, we must adopt God's encouragement to Joshua. Sister, the task of taking Canaan is upon us. Now is the time to move forward without fear.

WRAPPING UP

Joshua 1–6 details the specifics of the Israelites' triumphal entry into Canaan. At the end of each lesson this week, I'm going to direct your attention to specific passages from this section of Scripture. The goal will be to determine how the theme for the day played a critical role in the Hebrews' entrance into the promised land. Read the following excerpts and then explain how "being strong and courageous" played a necessary factor for success in each situation.

Rahab—Joshua 2:15-24

The Priests—Joshua 3:6,15-16

Day 2
Willingness to Take Your Post

As war with the Amalekites became imminent, Moses assigned responsibilities for the upcoming battle. Imagine how Joshua felt as he stood before Moses. His eyes must have been wide with wonder as he heard the assignment he was being given. Moses, flanked on either side by Aaron and Hur, was the aged leader explaining that only one of their foursome would physically enter the coming conflict.

Read Exodus 17:8-13. In the margin list the task assigned to each person.

Moses:

Aaron:

Hur:

Joshua:

Moses' brother Aaron and a man named Hur directly assisted the leader of God's people. Their prestigious job not only kept them out of the battle but also gave them the appearance of importance. Their role seemed far more "spiritual" than Joshua's practical assignment of drawing battle plans, motivating troops, and risking his life. They would hold Moses' arms to the heavens as he sought God for victory.

Historical credit for the victory would go to the two holding up Moses' hands and not Joshua's keen planning. Joshua's job not only seemed less impressive; his task was far more dangerous. Yet Joshua didn't dispute the calling, try to renegotiate, or even attempt to trade his post for another. Willingly he accepted the role God planned for him, even when it may have seemed less pleasant or even less spiritual than those tasks assigned Aaron and Hur. However, Aaron's and Hur's job did not outweigh their upcoming leader's. Both Joshua's dirty, perilous, and hands-on assignment and these men's determination to steady Moses' arms led to victory.

What tasks to which you are currently called don't always feel as worthwhile as you could wish? Why?

As we move forward in our spiritual journeys with God, we must answer the question, "Will we accept our posts?" I'm not referring to the duty or assignment you might receive at another stage in life. I'm asking you to answer the question in regard to what God wants to do through you today.

Often we become so consumed with envy over what God asks someone else to do that we fail to get around to what God asks of us. We allow our eyes to divert to the assignments of others, taking our focus off the task at hand. Since promised-land living is largely about knowing, accepting, and doing God's will for us, we must heed Joshua's example. He willingly, without complaint or fuss, fulfilled the role appointed to him.

Have you ever felt God's task for you is less appealing, less safe, or even less spiritual than the tasks He appoints to others? While you watch others lead worship, teach Bible studies, go to seminary, or serve in ways that seem "high-on-the-hill-of-holiness," do you feel frustrated by your own role within the church and in your life?

In the margin note some of necessary tasks that don't always seem worthwhile to God's kingdom?

Changing diapers, working at your corporate job, helping an elderly person shop for groceries, or just fighting life's battles with a Christian mind-set may seem meaningless and overwhelming, especially when you compare them with what others get to do. It can be difficult to stay focused on our task when credit for the victory often goes to others while we fight over-looked battles. We must come to understand that the task God has given us in this season of our lives is just as important to the health of the church as leading missions programs and singing solos in the church choir.

My friend Renee struggles with the current role she's been assigned in Christ's body. She desires to serve in full-time church ministry, but the only jobs she can find are administrative in nature. She enjoys what she does but struggles with feeling that the Lord's work can't be done through her in a simple position like this one. She's hardly alone in her struggles.

In the margin beside each of the following examples note why the woman might feel insignificant in her current role, and how she can serve Christ's body through her circumstances.

Bernadette received training to direct an adult-education ministry, but she can't afford to give up her job as a manager in a family-owned restaurant.

Laura signed up as a volunteer for the women's conference at her church. She just got her assignment in the mail; she's on bathroom duty.

Chelsea longs for children. She's been married 12 years, and the doctor told her she should consider adoption. She's unable to conceive.

Angela led a women's Bible study for eight years. While she hopes to teach larger groups, her study has a steady attendance of about 25.

Leigh is a single mom who can barely find time to think straight much less make time for local ministry.

Gina's husband passed away, leaving her alone in a huge home with a lot of things she can't use. She wonders how she can minister to younger couples without her husband's help.

BODY PARTS

As I write this lesson, I am five months pregnant with my third child. During the first trimester, certain foods made my stomach cramp. I found that when my stomach was upset, my entire body felt bad. Just because one body part wasn't functioning well, my whole body required rest before I could go on with my day. Amazing how the failure of one part of the body to do what it was created to do can hamper the entire body from functioning effectively. The apostle Paul seems to agree. In 1 Corinthians 12:14-27, he used the illustration of the human body to explain how all believers are equally important to building up God's spiritual body.

Read 1 Corinthians 12:1,4-31. Then answer the following questions T for true and F for false.

_____ Everyone has the same spiritual gifts (vv. 4-7).
_____ Only some believers are given spiritual gifts (v. 7).
_____ Spiritual gifts are given for the common good of the entire body of Christ (v. 7).
_____ Spiritual gifts are given to believers as the Spirit sees fit (v. 11).
_____ All gifts are equally necessary and valuable (vv. 22-23).

The Spirit gives spiritual gifts to all believers in Jesus Christ. God designed each gift to enable a believer to accomplish His calling on her life. When a believer exercises her gift, she builds and encourages the entire body. Since every gift is necessary, none is more important or critical than another. God uses all of our gifts as we allow Him to work through us. Contentment with our circumstances comes as we rest in and utilize the gifts God provides.

Think of a person who might feel that what she is doing is insignificant in God's kingdom. List why her activity is so important to the body of Christ. Call her and thank her for her work. Make sure to share your list with her.

WHY ME? WHY NOW?

If called from my quiet life of relative obscurity to start selecting an army to exact vengeance on a formidable foe, I, unlike Joshua, may have questioned not only the calling but my ability to fulfill it. After all, even if Joshua knew he had the gift of military leadership, defeating the menacing Amalekites was no small undertaking. Even as I sharpened my sword for battle, "Why me?" and "Why now?" would surely come out of my mouth.

Moses' selection and support of Joshua might have played a part in building his confidence. Despite Joshua's lack of military training, Moses saw potential in the young man that Joshua may not have seen in himself. Moses realized that this task would prove Joshua's ability and prepare him for future conquests. God uses our current experiences to prepare us for what's ahead.

Moses saw Joshua's potential and called him to act on it. Has anyone ever seen in you something you did not see in yourself? How did their belief in you affect your attitude and effort toward the job you'd been asked to do? One of the best things we can do as believers who want all that God has for us is to trust that God knows the answers to our *why me?* and *why now?* questions.

"Before I formed you in the womb I knew you, And before you were born I consecrated you; I have appointed you a prophet to the nations."
Jeremiah 1:5

How does Jeremiah 1:5 answer the question why me?

How does Ecclesiastes 3:1-8 answer why now?

Prior to our births, the Lord purposes specific roles for us in His kingdom's work. Throughout our lives, we'll fill those roles in His perfect timing. You and I don't need to waste energy formulating our own answers to life's questions. Instead, we can refocus that energy to determine our spiritual gifts and discover how we can best use those talents and abilities to edify and strengthen His body, the church. Whatever our specific calling in this specific moment, we must grow satisfied and confident in our God-given ability to handle it.

The success of God's people depends on the Joshuas, the Aarons, and the Hurs all doing their parts for the glory of God. Do a quick heart-check: Are you assisting or detracting from the body of Christ's ability to function well? To experience all that God has for us and for the church to experience all that God has for her, we must be willing to take our posts.

WRAPPING UP

Please read the following passages and describe how a willingness to take on the assigned post was imperative to each person's successful entry into Canaan. Ask the Lord to give you a holy courage to accept your post. Promised-land living depends on it.

Joshua: Joshua 1:1-2

Reubenites, Gadites, and Manasseh: Joshua 1:12-16

The Children of Israel: Joshua 3:3-4

Day 3
The Minority Report

Standing alone or with just a few can make it increasingly difficult to stand your ground and maintain your belief in God. Joshua knew this all too well. The second major endeavor in which Joshua is highlighted is found in Numbers 13. When Moses and the people came to the edge of Canaan at Kadesh-barnea, the Lord allowed Moses to select men from each of the 12 tribes to spy out the promised land. Suddenly, Joshua found himself in the uncomfortable minority.

Read Numbers 13:18-20. What were the spies sent to discover about: the people, the land, the cities?

A quick glance at Deuteronomy 1:22 reveals that God allowed Moses to send the spies because it is what the Hebrew children wanted. They desired the spies to examine not merely the best route to enter Canaan but to determine whether to enter it at all. "The implication given," one commentator explains, "was that if the land looked impregnable, the decision of Moses should be to forego assault."[2] The problem with this approach was that God had already given them a specific word regarding Canaan: He would give it to them (see Num. 13:1-2). The people's desire to test out Canaan's bounty, people, and fortifications revealed a mistrust of God. Joshua stood in the midst of millions who were questioning God.

Several years ago God began speaking to me about the spiritual inheritance He planned for my life. As I asked more questions and got more answers, God made it increasingly apparent that I needed to make some tough decisions regarding my willingness to accept His plans even when others balked. Over the months my search for abundant relationship with God through His precious Spirit has taken me into uncharted territory. When discouraged by well-meaning Christians who questioned my eagerness to experience more of God, I repeatedly asked myself, *Will I stay where I am spiritually, growing complacent and apathetic to God's voice,* or *will I trust God with my journey and my relationships along the way?*

Against whom or what might you have to bravely stand to embrace God's promises to you?

> The ten saw God, if at all, only through the difficulties of the situation. These two men saw the difficulties through God. In one case the difficulties minimized God. in the other, God minimized the difficulties.[3]

If you listed specific names, about whom are you most concerned and why? Ask a group member to pray with you about how the Lord will deal with that relationship.

Only Joshua and Caleb chose to trust God at His word. Their determination to believe plunged the two into the minority. I've discovered a common link in those who most impact me. They stand in an obvious minority. They work against the grain of the culture and sometimes against other Christians in their own spheres of influence to more fully embrace God's activities in their lives.

While some might choose to enjoy questionable forms of entertainment, to halfheartedly adhere to spiritual disciplines, or to stay in the "safe-zone" of comfortable Christianity, these people choose to believe God though they must sometimes stand alone to do it.

Which of the following areas we've studied will likely thrust you into the minority? Check all that apply.
- leaving the lure of Egypt behind me
- expecting miracles
- anticipating God's manifest presence
- taking God at His word
- stepping out in faith before I see proof of God's activity
- other: _____

Explain your answer.

BELIEVING GOD

Conquering Canaan will require a lifelong commitment to courage, our posts, and our position in the minority. Taking God at His word isn't popular. With growing disrespect for the Scriptures and a swelling disregard for hearing God's voice, few people celebrate a desire to adopt a radical lifestyle faith. When it appears that everything in the natural realm opposes God's Word, a minority stand seems overwhelmingly pointless. That's why it's so important that our faith remain rooted in the facts of God's promises to us. This maneuver will protect us from the enemy's attempts to discourage us and take our hearts off the prize.

> **Read Numbers 13:27-28 in the margin. Circle what the spies found that validated God's promise to them. Underline things that caused them to question God.**
>
> **Read Joshua's and Caleb's words to Israel in Numbers 14:7-9. How do you think faith influenced their perception of the land?**
>
> **How did the spies' conclusion clash with Joshua's and Caleb's?**

"Thus they told him, and said, 'We went in to the land where you sent us; and it certainly does flow with milk and honey, and this is its fruit. Nevertheless, the people who live in the land are strong, and the cities are fortified and very large; and more over, we saw the descendants of Anak there.' "
Numbers 13:27-28

Each time I read the spies' majority report, I'm stunned by the fact that though they held Canaan's fruit in their hands, they could not comprehend that God planned to give the land to them. Even after receiving bounty that they could touch and even taste, the Israelite spies spent more time and energy focusing on the possibility of defeat than on God's promise of victory.

> **In the chart below, record three things you believe God has asked you to believe Him for in your life. On the other side, list things that make it difficult for you to trust.**

I should believe God for …	Things opposing my trust …

Understand that the fruit the Israelites held served as proof of God's credibility. Yet even with this fresh testimony of God's goodness and trustworthiness, the spies aired a laundry list of reasons to abort the Canaan invasion. Even as they whined, proof of milk and honey went uncelebrated. Catching sight of the opposition they'd face caused them to question their belief in God.

Doubt sees
the obstacles.

Faith sees the way!

Doubt sees the
darkest night,

Faith sees the day!

Doubt dreads
to take a step.

Faith soars on
high!

Doubt questions,
"Who believes?"

Faith answers, "I!"[5]

Revisit the last activity. For each entry, determine whether you usually place more weight on the right or left side. To help you visualize your tendencies, put a check mark on the corresponding side of the chart.

The spies said, "We are not able to go up against the people, for they are too strong for us" (Num. 13:31). Their negativity spread like wildfire among the people, tainting the hearts and minds of the millions. Choosing to listen to the voices of defeat, the people felt hopeless.

Joshua and Caleb knew that while the Israelites couldn't overtake Canaan on their own, God could through them. The same is true for us. We can't conquer life's trials on our own, but God allows us to overcome with His help.

Sadly, many believers tend to give more weight to their fears than the supernatural power of God. Consider my friend Sharon's story. Sharon has been my friend for over 20 years. Recently diagnosed with an incurable illness for which the doctors recommended several medications to ease her pain and delay progression, Sharon hesitated to follow the doctors' advice. With the prescriptions came a long list of unpleasant side effects. Feeling overwhelmed, Sharon spent hours talking to the Lord about what He would have her to do. Over time she felt confident that God wanted her to believe that He could take care of her health without the aid of medicines. Through a series of circumstances, God confirmed His word to her. Armed with little more than her faith, Sharon decided not to take the prescriptions.

Difficulty came though when Sharon's friends and family found out about her decision. Negativity descended on her like a cloud. Though God gave Sharon many "fruits" to show for His promise to her regarding her health, she was constantly under pressure to stand up to the negatives others kept fresh in her mind. Daily she chooses to trust God's promise to care for her above the opposition's assurance that He won't.

My friend's decision to not take the medication is not for everyone; however, her resolve to stand on God's Word is. While Sharon's family and friends have valid concerns from a human perspective, they don't take into account that God is not bound by human methods and means. Remember, the spies' report wasn't fictitious. The cities did prove fortified, and the inhabitants were fierce. The problem with the report was that the spies allowed valid concerns to weigh more heavily than God's word and their confidence in it.

My sister, when we submit only to the physically observable and to the judgment and advice offered in this world, we lose sight of God. We must not live as people more directed by human reasoning than by faith.

TRUSTING

Failing to trust God doesn't happen in a split second. When we neglect our faith, we do so because we've allowed a series of observations and decisions to lead us there. In his book *Joshua*, Phillip Keller gives the stages of the believer's decision-making that lead to spiritual deterioration: "Following just facts leads one down a dangerous, slippery trail that can end only in failure," he states. Keller identifies the four fatal steps as facts, fear, fantasy of foreboding, and failure.[4] Here's how I see each step:

1. Facts—always look unbeatable and discouraging.
2. Fear—implanted by the Enemy.
3. Fantasy of foreboding—creating a "what if" scenario.
4. Failure—refusal to carry out God's plan.

In other words, we don't stay true to our faith when we allow the "facts" to discourage us and bind us in fear. As we consider the possibilities of what might go wrong if we step out and do as God says, we slowly convince ourselves that the possibility of the negative is more trustworthy than God. Then we often convince ourselves not to carry out what the Lord asks.

Scan Numbers 13–14. Briefly explain how the spies illustrate Keller's fatal steps to disaster. Note how each stage led to the next.

fear   fantasy of foreboding

facts   failure to do God's will

Numbers 14:37-38 explains that the spies who followed the steps to disaster "died by a plague before the LORD." Only "Joshua the son of Nun and Caleb the son of Jephunneh remained alive out of those men who went to spy out the land." We must hold fast to our trust in the Lord even if it means being in the minority. Without it, we'll miss the abundance Christ longs to give.

End today by discovering how the principles became key to the success of Joshua's life. Notice how it drastically impacted the invasion of Canaan.

Rahab—Joshua 2:10-15

Joshua and the Hebrews—Joshua 6:3-5,10,20

Day 4
Boots Made for Walking

This past week my father and pastor, Dr. Tony Evans, gave a stirring illustration. He recalled a time when the church, with less than 100 members, had barely enough money to cover expenses, much less anything extra. God called the church to expand its facilities in the midst of those trying times.

Dad explained that even though the church's financial outlook seemed bleak, he knew in his heart that the church would one day own a particular strip of land. In a physical demonstration of his faith in God's word to him, Dad walked up and down the road along the edge of that promised property. He talked to the Lord as he walked and set out to plant his feet on every part of the acreage he felt God intended the church to own.

"Every place on which the sole of your foot treads, I have given it to you."
Joshua 1:3

Today Oak Cliff Bible Fellowship ministers to the community from that 66-acre piece of land my father walked. A sanctuary, youth center, elementary and middle school, community outreach building, and pregnancy care center stand in what was once an empty field. The buildings stand as testimony to the fact that one man heard God, believed Him, and chose to walk on what God promised.

Joshua knew God called him to take Canaan by force. Nevertheless, he recognized that the land was a gift from Yahweh, an inheritance long promised to the people.

The Hebrews had access to all of God's gift, but the promised land didn't belong to them until they physically walked on it. Repeatedly, the Hebrews had to rely on God's help to claim new ground. If they only ventured one mile into Canaan, that's all the territory they owned. If they only traveled 10 miles inside the promised boundaries, then only 10 miles lay at their disposal. They couldn't just think about, dream about, pray about, or hope for Canaan at its fullest. Only if they spent their lives consistently pressing onward to conquer more of the land could they claim their entire inheritance. God required the Hebrews to lace up their spiritual boots and actively, continually walk out in faith.

What's the difference between passive faith and active faith?

How might believers balance waiting on God and moving forward in faith?

Group Discussion: How is walking in faith different from "name it-claim it" theology?

AS MUCH AS YOU WANT

In the time of Abraham God set aside every part of Canaan as an inheritance for His people (see Gen. 12:1-7). Because of that promise not one square inch of Canaanite territory belonged to Israel's enemies. However, God allowed the Hebrews to fully embrace the promised land only as they actively participated in its conquest.

Like the Israelites, you and I must put one foot in front of the other to show our faith in what God says. Thinking about, talking about, or even praying about our spiritual inheritance will not cause us to acquire it. I'm not suggesting we put on our literal walking shoes like my father did and set out on a physical march, but I am suggesting that we take practical steps to daily illustrate our faith in God.

Choose two of the following Scripture illustrations and answer the corresponding questions.

The Resurrection of Lazarus—John 11:1-46
- In what way did Jesus require onlookers to participate in Lazarus's resurrection (v. 39)?
- What reason did Martha offer as to why Jesus' instructions might prove unpleasant (v. 39)?
- How did onlookers respond to Jesus' request (v. 41)?
- Had you been a participant in this situation, would you have responded to Jesus' instructions more like Martha or the onlookers? Why?

Bartimaeus—Mark 10:46-52
- What did the blind man do to show faith in Christ's ability to heal him (vv. 47-48)?
- What did Jesus ask him to do? How did Bartimaeus respond to Christ's request (vv. 49-50)?
- When discouraged by others in your walk with God, do you tend to respond persistently like Bartimaeus or to succumb to the pressure? What do you think this response might indicate about your level of faith?

Healing a Nobleman's Son—John 4:46-53
- How did the child's father show active faith (vv. 47,50)?
- How was his active faith rewarded (vv. 51-52)?
- Which of the following best describes how you would respond in a situation similar to this father's?
  - ▨ I would take God at His word and walk back home to see my healthy son.
  - ▨ I would wait for some type of proof that my son was healed before leaving.
  - ▨ I would demand that Jesus come to my house and lay hands on my child.
  - ▨ I don't think I'd have the courage to ask Jesus for help.

God requires our participation in securing His promises. Don't misunderstand: Our participation does not minimize God's ability. He doesn't need our help. He expects us to help so that we might grow in our faith and better appreciate His provision. If we want access to our full inheritance, we have to engage in an active faith that illustrates our belief in God's ability and moves forward in full confidence. Start believing and acting like He is who is says He is and can accomplish exactly what He said He will.

> On page 131 you wrote something God has called you to that requires a holy courage for you to accomplish. In the margin write the practical steps you can take to show an active faith in God's ability to accomplish His promises in your life.

WALKING IN THE SPIRIT

Living with an active faith requires two things. The most obvious is courage to act on God's promises regardless of what others think or say. The second and most important is the development of a keen ability to correctly hear God's voice.

Our spiritual inheritance is recorded in the pages of Scripture. We must weigh anything we think we hear God say against the authority of His written Word. When it comes to more personal matters that apply specifically to your life, you must discern the voice of God so that you act only on what God really says. We can't just decide what we want God to do, act on it, and then get frustrated when He doesn't respond to us as we'd like. Instead, we must wait to hear God's voice, weigh what we think we hear against Scripture and then follow God's leading. This process is called walking by the Spirit.

When Moses asked God to reveal his successor, God showed him Joshua. What distinguishing characteristic made Joshua suitable for the job? (Num. 27:18).

God pointed out that while others might allow fear or the lure of idolatry to distract them from the mission, Joshua was trustworthy. Why? Because God's Spirit was within him.

Read Joshua 1:8. What action did Joshua need to take to "have success"?
- sharpen his sword and reinforce his shield
- hold a prayer meeting in his tent
- meditate on God's Word

"So the LORD said to Moses, 'Take Joshua the son of Nun, a man in whom is the Spirit, and lay your hand on him.' "
Numbers 27:18

According to Ephesians 1:13-14, you and I are suitable for the job of claiming our rightful inheritance because our salvation includes a gift, and it's the same one Joshua had: the Holy Spirit. He guides and empowers us to accomplish God's work. Our task, much like Joshua's, is to daily tune into the Spirit's guidance by searching the Word, submitting to Him in obedience, and relying on His power to accomplish what we are asked to do. We can do anything when we allow Him to work through us.

According to Galatians 5:16, what are we supposed to do "by the Spirit"?

"Walk by the Spirit, and you will not carry out the desire of the flesh."
Galatians 5:16

The verb used in Galatians 5:16 is *peripateo*. It translates "to tread all around, walk (about)." The implication here is that the Christian life requires perpetual spiritual motion. Success in claiming what's rightfully ours is accomplished only when we depend on the Spirit for each step of the journey.

Spiritual walking is much like physical walking. Both learned skills require us to shift full weight to one limb at a time. Just as we learn to allow our left leg to handle our body's weight as we lift our right leg, we manage spiritual walking only when placing full confidence in the Holy Spirit's ability to support us along the way. Although the Spirit is in each believer's life, you claim your spiritual inheritance only to the extent that you walk in faith on it.

Remember, walking by the Spirit requires lifelong commitment. The territory conquered and possessed in the time of Joshua was much less than what was promised Abraham in the Book of Genesis. Expanding Israel's borders required years of moving forward against opposition followed by continual refortification and defense of God's gift. Though the Hebrews eventually saw their territory drastically increase under the leadership of King

David, they still have not received the full measure of their inheritance. Worse, their disobedience eventually caused them to lose access to the promised land entirely. Prophecy assures us, however, that the land will be gloriously and fully returned to them at Christ's coming (see Jer. 16:14-15; Amos 9:11-15; Zech. 8:4-8).

As believers who want to claim what is rightfully ours, we must take steps of faith by the Spirit's power until we see Christ face-to-face. Our spiritual success depends on it.

As we wrap up today, consider how an active faith was critical to these people.

Joshua—Joshua 1:9-11

the Hebrews—Joshua 3:5

the Priests—Joshua 3:15-16

Rahab's loved ones—Joshua 6:23

Day 5
Leader of the Pack

Christopher Columbus bravely explored and conquered the New World. Basing his expedition on sailors' speculation that land lay further west than anyone traveled, he set out to find that "world" based solely on a hope that it existed. Columbus's confidence and certainty of success were so contagious that he actually convinced family members, sailors, and ultimately the Spanish king and queen to support his efforts to find new territory. The astonishing results of his first journey with just 3 ships led to securing 17 boats just to carry all those who wanted to accompany him. Each of his four voyages explored new territory and further aroused interest and curiosity. Soon, even Columbus's most intense critics believed in a land they had never seen.

Armed with our faith in God's Word, our promised inheritance, and a bold courage to press past the security of our religious comfort zones, you and I daily traverse new spiritual ground in our personal lives. As we continue to set foot on new territory, the interest and curiosity of other believers will ignite. When others see God operating in our lives, they'll want to embark on new faith expeditions of their own. I believe God ordained your participation in this study to prepare you to lead others. Your exploration of new spiritual ground should spread among your circle of influence as you commit to encourage others to venture into new territory with God.

List three people you hope will join you in claiming their full inheritance.

Take a moment to pray for them. Lift each name up to the Father, and ask Him to allow something in you to spark their desire for more of God.

CONVICTED TO CONVINCED

Joshua knew he needed to share his experiences with the Lord with others. After receiving personal encouragement and instruction (Josh. 1), Joshua set out to convince a crowd of millions that their years of waiting in the wilderness were over. Remember, 38 years earlier Joshua received a view of Canaan that he could not forget. He remembered Canaan's ripe fruit and the richness of the land. He knew firsthand that Canaan was just as wonderful as God promised (Num. 13). With those delightful memories in mind, Joshua desired to share a small taste of Canaan with the people. He wanted Canaan's bounty and proof of the Lord's goodness fresh in their minds too.

Shortly before beginning the Canaan conquest, Joshua sent two spies into the land to get a report that would help them plan their invasion. When the spies returned, they explained what they'd seen and experienced, including details of their scare in Jericho (Josh. 2:23). Years earlier Moses had entertained the requests of those who did not want to risk entry into Canaan but Joshua handled things differently.

According to Joshua 3:1, what did Joshua do after hearing the spies' reports?
- called a town meeting to discuss everyone's opinion.
- decided to wait a while longer before entering Canaan
- rose early to obey God's command

As a man of conviction Joshua was confident that God would act on His word, finally enabling the people to come into their inheritance. Because of his conviction to follow hard after God, approximately two million refugees were convinced to move themselves and everything they owned the seven miles from Shittim to the edge of the Jordan. There they prepared to cross the raging flood waters of the Jordan River (Josh. 3:1).

My sister, you and I will convince others to experience God only to the measure that we follow the conviction His Spirit has stirred in us. With that in mind, we need to grow fully convinced of these things:

Are you fully convinced that:
- **Our wilderness journeys are not a mistake but God's chosen pathways to inheritance.**　　yes　no　maybe
- **God will provide protection and guidance for us during our wilderness journeys.**　　yes　no　maybe
- **We can expect to see God perform miracles and demonstrate His presence to us along the way.**
  　　yes　no　maybe
- **We can live in an abundant place of divine milk (satisfaction) and honey (sweetness).**
  　　yes　no　maybe

I became a Christian at a young age but was never fully convicted in my own heart that I could encounter the fullness of God in my everyday living. I never thought I could personally experience God's power and hear His voice. In hindsight I realize that lack of conviction kept me from having active faith like Joshua's. A noncontagious, lackluster spirituality resulted.

I found in those years that it didn't matter how much I talked about my faith with others or encouraged them in their relationships with the Lord; they didn't see anything about my life that spurred them forward in their own walks with God. Only after I began to experience God personally did others begin to question me about my relationship with Jesus and desire it for themselves. Now I'm repeatedly amazed to hear others, even initial critics, asking about God simply because of what they see Him doing in me.

Whose relationship with God whets your appetite for more in your own relationship with the Lord?

What about their conviction helped to convince you?

I hope that during our six weeks together I've given you a glimpse of God's milk and honey. I want you to expect His manifest presence. I want you to experience milk and honey as you see God work. As you see His miracles, do what Joshua did: invite others to see God's goodness for themselves. Let your confidence in God shine as a light that increases others' determination to follow after Him.

MAKING DISCIPLES

As a little girl, I remember hearing the legendary story of the woman at the well. In John 4 this Samaritan sister was drawing water from the town's well when a Jewish man walked up to her and started talking. This was odd not only because Samaritans and Jews didn't get along but also because women were usually looked down on and ignored by men. The ensuing conversation between the two forever altered the woman's life as she became aware that Jesus was no ordinary man. Before their meeting, she'd known a Messiah was coming (John 4:25) and awaited His arrival. Jesus' explanation that He was the Christ, however, rocked her world.

    My childhood Sunday School lessons always ended somewhere around this critical point. Only in recent years have I understood the gravity of what took place after this woman encountered Jesus.

"So the woman left her water-pot, and went into the city and said to the men, 'Come, see a man who told me all the things that I have done; this is not the Christ, is it?' They went out of the city, and were coming to Him."
John 4:28-30

> **Read John 4:28-30. What did the woman do after meeting Jesus?**

> **What is interesting about her audience's demographic?**

> **How did they respond to her claims that she had met the Christ?**

According to verse 39, a little revival broke out among the Samaritans who met Jesus. Largely because of this woman's personal conviction, many people from the city became convinced that Jesus was the Messiah. When they came to see Jesus and listened to Him for themselves, they started their own spiritual expeditions. In fact, they said to the woman whose testimony introduced them to Christ, "It is no longer because of what you said that we believe, for we have heard for ourselves and know that this One is indeed the Savior of the world" (John 4:42). Their spiritual encounter with the Messiah

149

may have begun because they heard what He had done for her, but now they had experienced Him personally.

This is what we are after: hearing others say, "My interest in the Lord may have started with what you had to say about Him, but now I know for myself!"

Consider the names of the people you listed in today's first activity. What are some practical ways you can encourage someone to "cross the Jordan River" and enter into promised-land living?

"Go therefore and make disciples of all the nations, baptizing them in the name of the Father and the Son and the Holy Spirit."
Matthew 28:19

God puts people in our paths who will find spiritual encouragement in what they see happening in us. While some might positively respond to a simple spoken message about Christ, others won't seek God until they find a Christ-follower whose life positively intrigues them. Our goal, then, should always be to "let [our] light[s] shine before men in such a way that they may see [our] good works, and glorify [our] Father who is in heaven" (Matt. 5:16).

WRAPPING UP

Read the following passages and explain how a commitment to positive influence became crucial in the crossing of the Jordan River and entrance into Canaan.

How did Joshua influence the people?—Joshua 1:16-18

How did the people respond to the priest's leadership?— Joshua 3:14-17

How did Rahab influence her family?—Joshua 6:23

1. *Webster's New World College Dictionary,* 4th Edition (Foster City, CA: IDG Books Worldwide, 2001), 333.
2. Irving L. Jensen. *Numbers: Journey to God's Rest-Land* (Chicago: Moody, 1964), 60.
3. James Hastings, D.D. *The Greater Men and Women of the Bible, Moses–Samson* (New York: Charles Scribner's Sons, 1914), 370.
4. W. Phillip Keller. *Joshua: Man of Fearless Faith* (Waco, TX: Word Books, 1983), 41.
5. Paul Lee Tan. *Encyclopedia of 7700 Illustrations: A Treasury of Illustrations, Anecdotes, Facts and Quotations for Pastors, Teachers and Christian Workers.* Garland TX : Bible Communications, 1996.

LEADER GUIDE

Overview and course design

This guide provides directions for a seven-session group study. A leader kit is also available, containing the video messages to be used during the group sessions. The video sessions may also be purchased from *lifeway.com* as digital downloads. Though you can do the study using only the print, it is designed to watch the video teaching sessions and then do the print study.

Group sessions require a minimum of one hour, preferably 90 minutes for adequate discussion time. Some groups may choose a more flexible schedule such as viewing and discussing the video one week and discussing the print study the next. Note the varying video session lengths from 29 to 50 minutes. By design the wrap-up session is brief. Your group will complete their study in the workbook. Then the final session is a review and a personal word of encouragement and appreciation to the group. You may choose to use the bonus video segments as a fun way to conclude the study with your group.

If your group is too large for effective group discussion, watch the video as a large group. Then do your discussion in smaller groups. Enlist and prepare small group leaders. This guide is primarily for the small group facilitator.

Beginning a Bible Study Group

- Pray for God's leadership; ask for His help in all arrangements, including bringing to the study those people who have a hunger to press forward in their walk with God.
- Reserve your meeting place and time. Arrange for childcare if needed.
- Promote the study in your church and community. The promotional video segments can be used for in-church promotion as well as broadcast on local television. Your may choose to offer an opportunity for women to preregister for the study to get a preliminary count. Have member books available for participants at the first small-group session.
- Arrange to have a DVD player in your meeting room each week.
- Enlist group facilitators for the number of groups you anticipate.

Responsibilities of Facilitators

Prayer

Pray for your group as a whole, for individual members, for your leadership of the group, and that members will hear and obey God.

Time and Preparation

Honor participants time by beginning and ending on time. Be prepared to facilitate the group. Complete each week's assignments and preview the video sessions. You do not have to have all the answers, but you need to be familiar with the content. Before the first session look through the entire book to familiarize yourself with the content and Bible study method. Review the introduction and be ready to explain to group members what they can expect from the study.

Safe Discussion Group

Establish a safe learning and sharing environment where no one is intimidated and no one dominates the group.

Lead the Sessions

Let the group know you will facilitate the session—not lecture—and that you don't know everything about the subject. You will guide the group as you help each other learn about the material they studied during the week.

Session One
Shackle Free

1. Have group members introduce themselves by sharing in one minute an interesting journey they've taken. Introduce yourself first and give members an example to follow.
2. Welcome members to the study. Pay particular attention to newcomers. Thank participants for their attendance.
3. Overview the course. Explain that the goal is life change, not just study. Their individual, daily study will begin the process of application and the small-group discussion will continue the process. Share that together you will discuss concepts you studied during the week, flesh out the concepts, and encourage each other on the journey.
4. Direct members to page 6 for the first session viewer guide. You have permission to copy the viewer guide pages for those who are visiting a session or who are deciding if they want to join the group.
5. Watch video session 1 [36:41], completing viewer guide on pages 6-7.

6. Discuss insights and challenges members gained from the session. Possible discussion questions include:

   a. How do you feel about joining in the quest to be one in a million?

   b. What do you think of when you think of abundance?

   c. What is the difference between perfection and satisfaction?

   d. From the list of promised-land living list Priscilla read (page 160) what two or three descriptions most appeal to you?

   e. How does the story of Jenny speak to you?

   f. What is the danger of Christianity as something you do?

   g. Have you ever placed faith in Christ for the remission of your sin? Are you hanging out in any of the places where the enemy reigns?

7. Encourage members to complete their study and to pray for each other daily. Dismiss with prayer.

Session Two
Welcome to the Wilderness

1. Greet and encourage members as they arrive. Open with prayer. Refer to your list of discussion questions. Share the page number as you ask each question so members can refer back to their responses. Possible questions include:

   a. Do you agree that many born-again believers never experience the fullness of God (p. 9)? If so, why?

   b. What adjectives would you use to describe the life of an individual living in bondage to sin (p. 11)?

   c. In what ways do you think lifestyle sin differs from original sin?

   d. Brainstorm in your group practical ways we can reprogram our thinking to fully enjoy God's freedom (p. 15).

   e. In a time when you became your own worst enemy, what did you say or think that impeded your spiritual progress (p. 18)?

   f. How do the strong flavors and smells of Egypt's food contribute to our bondage (p. 18)?

   g. What specific things is God asking you to leave behind so you can more closely follow Him (p. 20)?

   h. Brainstorm ways to guard yourself and your family from the trends that reflect the Enemy's work in our culture (p. 22).

2. Show session 2 video [29:40]. If time permits, discuss insights or challenges members gained from the session. Possible questions include:

   a. Why do you think God deliberately chooses the wilderness for us?

   b. What tempts us to hide our incredible nature and be like others?

c. How does it feel to be attending the "Oxford and Cambridge of God's students?"

d. How is the wilderness a favor God is doing for us?

3. Encourage group members to do their study this week. Close with prayer.

Session Three
EXPERIENCING GOD

1. Greet members. Open with prayer.

2. Lead discussion. Possible questions include:

a. When wilderness seasons come in your life or a friend's life, what or whom do you assume to be the source (p. 34)?

b. How would you feel if facing the desert on foot when a more convenient route obviously existed (p. 34)?

c. How does the fact that our trials have purpose alter your view of God's care (p. 35)?

d. Why do you think prioritizing intimacy with God can be difficult for today's Christian (p. 40)?

e. Do you have a $500 story to share with the group (p. 42)?

f. What are some practical ways that you remember God's goodness in lean times? Where do you see yourself in your walk with God right now (p. 43)?

g. What do you see as the toughest parts of your wilderness journey right now? What evidences so you see in the midst of it (p. 44)?

h. What have the frustrations and interruptions of the wilderness revealed to you about your heart's intentions (p. 45)?

i. If you found yourself in the Israelites' sandals in Exodus 15, how would you describe your attitude (p. 51)?

3. Show session 3 video [49:21]. If time permits, discuss. Possible questions:

a. How have you experienced being desensitized to some aspect of your relationship with God?

b. How does the unpredictability of God challenge you and how does it make you love Him?

c. In what circumstances do you need God's command not to fear?

d. What kinds of fears paralyze you if you don't trust God?

e. How do we want to do God's part instead of our part in situations?

f. How difficult do you find it to "stand there," to "be silent"?

4. Encourage group members to do their study this week. Close with prayer.

Session Four
SEEING HIM AT SINAI

1. Greet members. Open with prayer.
2. Lead discussion. Possible questions include:
   a. What is your definition of a miracle (p. 58)?
   b. How have you felt when God's directions seemed to be opposite the way you were headed (p. 59)?
   c. What are the dangers of looking back when encountering our "Red Seas" (p. 60)?
   d. Why do you think God allowed the Israelites to encounter undrinkable water (p. 62)?
   e. Have you ever felt frustrated or angry with God because of a disappointment (p. 64)?
   f. What kinds of lessons has God taught you and through what kinds of tests (p. 67)?
   g. How do you know when an inner hunger is for only God to fill, and what is the purpose of spiritual hunger (p. 68)?
   h. Why do you think God orchestrates in-between times in your spiritual life (p. 70)?
   i. When was a time your appreciation for God's ability deepened? How did it impact your pursuit of the Lord (p. 75)?
3. Show session 4 video [49:50]. If time permits, discuss. Possible questions:
   a. When has God been saying to you, "steady as you go"?
   b. What does it mean for you to yield to the wilderness?
   c. What is the difference between a relationship and an enterprise?
   d. How do you sense God alluring you into a deeper relationship?
   e. How can you adjust to the reality that God is wild about you?
4. Encourage group members to do their study this week. Close with prayer.

Session Five
BREAKING BARRIERS

1. Greet members. Open with prayer.
2. Lead discussion. Possible questions include:
   a. What priorities do you think have taken precedence over intimacy with God in Christianity today (p. 84)?
   b. When have you seen God during a trying season of life (p. 85)?
   c. What have you learned as a result of a difficult time in your life (p. 87)?
   d. How does Isaiah 59:2 shed light on how sin impacts God's plans for His children (p. 90)?

e. How would our lives be different if our covenant with God was conditional, and how does this affect your desire to pursue holiness (p. 91)?

f. How did you respond to the idea that God speaks (p. 94)?

g. How does the idea of hearing God for yourself impact you (p. 95)?

h. What is one step you could take to overcome complacency in hearing God (p. 96)?

i. When you encounter God's power, do you tend to run to Him or run away from Him (p. 100)?

j. Did you grow up in an environment that contributed to a healthy or unhealthy fear of God (p. 101)?

3. Show session 5 video [40:35]. If time permits, discuss. Possible questions:

a. What are the visible evidences that someone is experiencing the power of God in her life?

b. What do you think and feel when you hear the word destiny?

c. What is the difference between the wilderness and wandering in the wilderness?

d. How can the promised land look too risky?

e. What does the fact that the Israelites saw but still refused to obey say to you?

f. What is your "valley of Eschol cluster keeper"?

4. Encourage group members to do their study this week. Close with prayer.

Session Six
ASPIRING TO ABUNDANCE

1. Greet members. Open with prayer.

2. Lead discussion. Possible questions include:

a. From what has God delivered or been delivering you? In what ways has the wilderness developed you (p. 105)?

b. How does the term destiny correspond to Canaan (p, 106)?

c. What changes may you need to make to embrace God's journey for you (p. 109)?

d. What tasks take your attention from relationship with God (p. 113)?

e. Why do you think the Lord withheld entry to Canaan from Moses rather than a lesser punishment (p. 116)?

f. In what way does your life mirror the character you chose (p. 119)?

g. What has God asked you to relinquish? What are the dangers of not letting go of the things God asks us to give up (p. 122)?

h. What things did you discover with the chart on page 125?

3. Show session 6 video [40:34]. If time permits, discuss. Possible questions:
   a. What kind of things have had to die for you to move on in your relationship with God?
   b. How important do you consider acting immediately in obedience?
   c. To what has God called you that you feel incapable and unequipped?
   d. How can you follow Jesus' example in John 5:19?
   e. In what ways do you give yourself to the good stuff instead of the God stuff?
   f. What difference might anticipating God's miracles make in your life? What do you need to do to sanctify yourself?
   g. What do you need to do to get your feet wet?

Session Seven
CONCLUSION

1. Greet members. Open with prayer.
2. Lead discussion. Possible questions include:
   a. What facets of promised-land living most stand out to you (p. 129)?
   b. What similarities do you see among the people who are enjoying God's inheritance (p. 130)?
   c. What do excuses regarding why you can't do what God asks reveal about how you view yourself (p.131)?
   d. What tasks to which you are currently called don't always feel as worthwhile as you could wish (p. 133)?
   e. How do you Joshua and Caleb's faith influenced their perception of the land (p. 139)?
   f. What are three things God has called you to believe Him for, and what makes it difficult to trust Him in those areas (p. 139)?
   g. How might believers balance waiting on God and moving forward in faith (p. 143)?
   h. What are some practical ways you can encourage someone else to "cross the Jordan River" and enter into promised-land living (p. 150)?
3. Show session 7 short video [7:33].
4. If you have time, either with this session or later, have a celebration of completing the study. You may use the bonus material as part of your celebration. Lead the group to plan ways they can continue to support one another in their journey.

Other Studies by Priscilla

DISCERNING THE VOICE OF GOD: HOW TO RECOGNIZE WHEN GOD SPEAKS
7 sessions

Discover the root to clear and daily communication with God—humble obedience. This revised and expanded edition includes fresh illustrations, articles from Dr. Tony Evans, and all-new video sessions.

Bible Study Book 005797596 **$12.99**
Leader Kit 005797597 **$149.99**

LifeWay.com/DiscerningTheVoiceOfGod

THE ARMOR OF GOD
7 sessions

The enemy always fails miserably when he meets a woman dressed for the occasion. Develop your own personalized strategy to secure victory against the enemy.

Bible Study Book 005727075 **$12.99**
Leader Kit 005727076 **$149.99**

LifeWay.com/ArmorOfGod

GIDEON: YOUR WEAKNESS. GOD'S STRENGTH.
7 sessions

The story of Gideon is one about God's love for His people. Learn to recognize your weakness as the key God gives you to unlock the full experience of His strength in your life.

Bible Study Book 005538485 **$12.99**
Leader Kit 005538484 **$149.99**

LifeWay.com/Gideon

JONAH: NAVIGATING A LIFE INTERRUPTED
7 sessions

Redefine interruption as God's invitation to do something greater than you could ever imagine. When Jonah was willing to allow God to interrupt his life, the result was city-wide revival.

Bible Study Book 005264295 **$12.99**
Leader Kit 005189429 **$149.99**

LifeWay.com/Jonah

DEVOTIONS WITH PRISCILLA AUDIO CD

A collection of 12 devotional teaching segments, each about 10 minutes long, taken from Priscilla's popular Bible studies. Listen while running errands, commuting to work, or exercising for a little on-the-go encouragement.

Audio CD Set 005271627 **$5.00**

LifeWay.com/PriscillaShirer
800.458.2772 | LifeWay Christian Stores
Pricing and availability subject to change without notice.

LifeWay | Wom

Going
BEYOND LIVE
with PRISCILLA SHIRER

Worship with ANTHONY EVANS

Find a City Near You at LifeWay.com/GoingBeyondLive

Going BEYOND SIMULCAST
with PRISCILLA SHIRER

Learn More About Hosting at LifeWay.com/GBSimulcast

LifeWay. Women | events

Event subject to change.
To register by phone for the Live event, call 800.254.2022.

PROMISED-LAND LIVING

These are some of the characteristics of a believer experiencing abundant life in Christ. While we will not achieve perfection in these areas on earth, they can be our overarching experience. Remember, the Israelites faced enemies as soon as they crossed the Jordan so promised-land living does not mean a life with no problems. It means experiencing God's power and presence in spite of difficulty. You know you are living in the land of abundance not when your circumstances change but when this list describes your life—even when circumstances have not changed.

- Senses and acknowledges God's continual presence—*Psalm 139:7-10*
- Is led by the Spirit of God—*Romans 8:14*
- Recognizes and tears down strongholds—*2 Corinthians 10:4*
- Separates physical and spiritual abundance—*Luke 12:15*
- Lives free from a lifestyle of sin—*Galatians 5:1; 1 Peter 2:24*
- Shows evidence of conformity to Christ's image—*Romans 8:29*
- Has confidence in her standing of righteousness before the Father —*Romans 8:1; 2 Corinthians 5:18-19;*
- Casts anxiety and worry on God—*1 Peter 5:7*
- Gives thanks in spite of difficult circumstances—*Philippians 4:6*
- Counts suffering for Christ as a blessing—*1 Peter 2:19-21*
- Displays divine power in weakness- 2 Corinthians 12:10
- Senses God's comfort and hope—*2 Thessalonians 2:16*
- Has confidence to draw near to God—*Hebrews 7:25; 10:19*
- Lives as an alien and stranger to this world—*1 Peter 2:11*
- Hears the voice of God—*John 10:27*
- Discerns the guidance of God's Spirit—*John 16:13*
- Believes God can supply her every need—*Philippians 4:13*
- Is open to receiving the gifts given by God's Spirit—*1 Corinthians 12:4-7*
- Recognizes and utilizes her spiritual gifts for the edification of Christ's body—*1 Peter 4:10; 1 Corinthians 4:7*
- Displays the fruit of God's Spirit in her daily living—*Galatians 5:22-23*
- Experiences consistent joy and peace—*John 15:11; Philippians 4:7*
- Rocognizes and utilizes God's spiritual armor—*Ephesians 6:10-18*
- Desires to know and do God's will—*Jeremiah 29:11; Ephesians 2:10*
- Expects that God is able to do more than she can ask or think —*Ephesians 3:20; 1 Corinthians 2:9*
- Anticipates seeing the miracles of God—*Galatians 3:5*
- Is content with what she has—*Philippians 4:12; Hebrews 13:5*
- Confesses sins and believes they are forgiven—*1 John 1:9*
- Values connection with the body of Christ—*Acts 2:46; Hebrews 10:25*
- Pursues unity in the body of Christ—*Ephesians 4:2-6; Romans 14:19*
- Forgives when wronged—*Matthew 18:21,22; Colossians 3:13*